Culturrific!

The Roadmap to a Terrific Experience Culture

BY

Matthew Hudson, PhD

Matthew Hudson

Twitter: @hudsonhead

**hudsonhead.com
buildanexperience.com**

The Menu

The Design Phase

Define Your Company Product   **page 135**

It's not about what are you selling, but what your customers are paying for.
- Define a company product.
- Learn how to define your company's product.

Cast Your Vision   **page 145**

An experience culture is values-driven.
- Learn the importance of a strong foundation of values and how to use it to set the stage for your employee's performance.
- Describe ways to discover your company values.
- Learn how to write a vision statement.
- Describe the role of a vision statement and how to make it work.

Craft Your Purpose   **page 159**

There is a difference between a vision statement and a purpose or mission statement.
- Learn their differences and significance of your service culture.
- Write your new purpose statement.
- More people know the mission statement to Star Trek than they do their own company's mission statement.

Create Your Experience Formula   **page 173**

Every business needs a formula for success that all of the employees in the organization can follow with ease and confidence. This is the only way to get the right service to happen on the front lines.
- Learn the elements of writing your experience formula.
- Benchmark formulas other companies have developed.

The Implementation Phase

Casting

The first place to start after you have engineered your plan is with your HR group and their hiring practices. They are pivotal to your change since they have so much influence within the company on matters that feed or "program" the culture.

- Learn to set the stage for all of your future employees, so they become assets to your new culture.
- Develop tools for recruiting.
- Learn to hire to fit your culture.
- Discuss how to write performer profiles for hiring correctly.
- Get tips on how to creatively hire and recast employees.

Training & Development

The most important ingredient, training serves as the catalyst to your culture change. This chapter sets the stage for the corporate university.

- Learn the principles of training in a service culture.
- Define the difference between teaching and training.
- Describe the training classes that must be developed for the culture change and how to run them.

Establishing a Learning University

A corporate university is much more than a neat logo on a sweatshirt; it's the vehicle to take your training where you need to go and one of the today's hottest buzzwords.

- Describe the five key elements of a corporate university.
- Define how to develop degree plans.
- Discuss ways to tie training to promotion and compensation.

Prelude

"Life is difficult."
- M. Scott Peck

"Culture change is harder."
- M. Hudson

Since this is the second edition of the book, I should probably start with an amazing story of epiphany that I had that led me to create a second version. But the truth is, my sister, Mindy, is the one who put me on the path.

I gave her a copy of my book when it first came out. She and her husband were opening a coffee roasting business, and I was their first investor. I told her the book would be a better guide than me since I lived in Texas and she was in Michigan.

Years, later, when their business started expanding and growing, she found that book sitting on a dusty shelf. She decided to read it (for the first time.) A couple of weeks after she started, I got a frantic phone call. "Oh my gosh!" Mindy shouted into the phone, "this book is like you are reading my mind. It's a roadmap of everything our business needs to do to be successful," she shared. "Why didn't I read this when you first gave it to me?"

Now reading this you probably think she's your sister, of course, she felt that way. Well, remember, she let the book sit on the shelf for many years before she read it, so this story is from a small business owner who just happens to be related to me.

Mindy's phone call opened my eyes. I had gone on and written other books and my focus had been taken away from corporate culture. The business world has changed dramatically since I first wrote this book and it needed an update. But what was special about the phone call was that Mindy proved that the principles in the book were sound and that its relevance was still true and needed.

Since the first edition of this book, online business and commerce have taken a sizeable share of the market and the instant access to information in the palm of our hands through our multiple mobile devices we each own has also shifted our habits and practices. And the generation of workers has changed from being dominated by Baby Boomers to a majority workforce of Millennials. **But even with all those shifts and changes, the principals of culture remain the same.**

In fact, as I researched in a preparation of writing this version, I found that the fundamental basics have not changed in corporate culture – only the players, the technology, and the speed. **And what's more fascinating is that "experience" is the most important word in business today and nothing drives experience better than a healthy corporate culture.**

While Denis Waitley was working on his doctorate, he wrote his dissertation on why people succeed. Earl Nightingale, who is considered to be the father of motivational speaking heard of Denis and read his dissertation. Earl convinced Denis to let him publish the work under the title "The Psychology of Winning."

My favorite Denis Waitley book is <u>Empires of the Mind.</u> Throughout the book, Denis gives various paradoxical proverbs to live by. My favorite one is this one that smacked me in the face and ego.

You must continue to gain expertise, but avoid thinking like an expert.

I may know my stuff, but so what? I was falling into the adage that knowledge is power. You will find out as you read this book that I don't believe this anymore. It's what you do with the knowledge that counts.

Denis is right. Arrogance and an unhealthy self-esteem are the only reasons that one would keep everything inside and think the world could not exist without them. I went into my profession because of the feeling I get when I see someone's eyes light up when they "get it" – that moment when they finally understand. When I can be instrumental in helping someone put the knowledge they already possess with a little of my own, I call that successful. I have always been taught that the measure of a man's success was not what he left to the world, but what he left in it.

And the truth is, as I've aged, I have come to understand that it's not how smart I am, it's how smart the people I know are. I have spent the last decade of my life traveling the world and listening to the best and brightest minds I could find. It is their wisdom and experiences that shape this book and not just mine. I have given over 2,000 keynote speeches during that time and the one truth I have come to accept is that there is more knowledge in the room than on the stage. **Arrogance has no place in the life of a servant.**

So what you are about to read is the process you must take to change your current corporate culture to an **experience culture**. Each step must be followed in sequence, and none should be rushed through. In fact, you have to read the whole book through first before you begin rolling it out in your company. If you try and do one piece at a time, it will fail. Been there and done that. So let me save you the time of making that mistake. Read everything through, so you see how they all connect first, then begin to work on each part step (stop) by step.

Each chapter is written so that it can be standalone. In my working with companies, I have found that it helps to have a section for each stakeholder (department) in the culture change process. The design of this book is such that you can hand out the one chapter that is written for that group or department. For example, the "Casting" chapter is written for your HR department.

Think if this more as a field guide than a textbook. As a matter of fact, if it starts to feel like a textbook, I'll quit! The last thing the world needs is another textbook. I'm not the "end all" authority on people. – Not even close. As I said, I'm just someone who has been blessed enough to travel the world and sit with some of the best and brightest minds and learn from their success and their mistakes.

The goal of this handbook is to help you keep from making the same mistakes either I have made, or I have seen others make or learned from other leaders' experiences. As you follow this guide, there will be times when you will be challenged. Expect it and prepare for it! What you do in this culture change process will not be easy and will push most of your employees and peers out of their comfort zone. And, we all know what happens when we do that!

I tried to write this book conversationally with free-standing chapters so that you can pull out the information you need without having to re-read the preceding chapters. References to points in other chapters are noted, though, in case you do need to review. We are not making you experts, but simply trying to convey the key steps and principles at play with culture change. I also make an attempt at humor throughout, but do not let this detract from the seriousness of the message. (A case in point is the obligatory pie chart.) Most of the names of the companies I have worked with have been left out due to client confidentiality.

The quotes at the beginning of each section and highlighted throughout are mine (unless otherwise dutifully noted), but you may feel free to use them as your own only if it results in you getting a promotion.

If you discover questions along the way, you may want to contact me. Our company, @hudsonhead, is a consulting practice dedicated to assisting companies with culture change – specifically those companies seeking to put an **experienced model** into place. As you read this book, if you see "we" it is referring to the people (outsiders and insiders) who I have worked with and continue to do so today on corporate culture. None of us is as strong as all of us.

Please email us your stories of success and strife to **matt@hudsonhead.com**.

Okay, no one likes long preludes. If you are like most, you skimmed this part anyway and are not even reading this sentence because you have skipped to chapter one. (If you didn't you would be rewarded because we numbered these pages as part of the total book instead of with Roman numerals or small letters of the alphabet so that you get full credit for all the pages read!) But if you haven't skipped there yet, we want you to turn to the last part of this book, the "Postlude." It is very important to start and end on a positive. We want you to keep the story in the "Postlude" in mind the entire time you are on this journey. It is one of my favorite stories from the life of Walt Disney.

You are a special person if you are deciding to change a culture. It takes courage, leadership, patience, and love to pull this off. I want you to know that I am behind you 100%. **Congratulations for making this decision.** Break a leg!

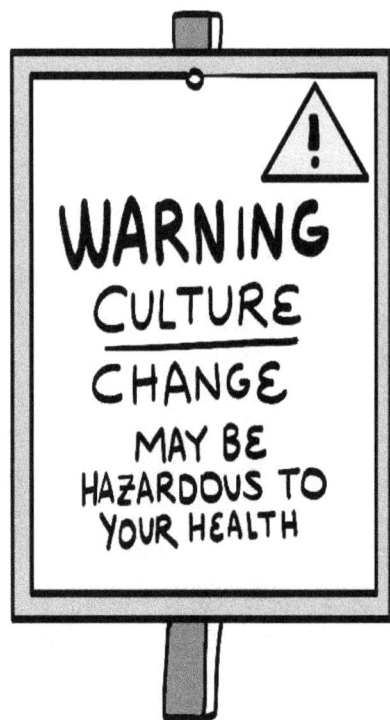

Chapter One

Culture change is not for the weak of heart!

Why are you doing this? Why are you deciding to make a change in your company's current culture? This is the operative question. I thought we would start this book with the reason I feel that all companies must take the journey on instilling an **experience culture**. My reason – competition.

Now you may read that last sentence and think, "well I'm not actually in competition with anyone. I am a non-profit organization." I hear you. But if you think you're not in competition I hate to break it to you, but you truly are. Other charities are courting every donor on your rolls, and their money could swiftly shift away. So, as you read these next parts, follow the principles and ideas as they can and do relate to your business – whether you are a non-profit, for-profit corporation, small business, family business or church. The principles and strategies you are about to read in this book, I have personally worked on and used with every type of company just listed.

It all started for me when I was a director of training in retail. I was working for an electronics retailer with many of the stores located in shopping malls. You remember shopping malls, the one-time wave of the future that has hit the rocks. Economists will argue that it was the soft economy, which slowed the traffic of malls; still, others will say it is the decline in disposable income.

Others say that it is the growth of category-killer superstores with a wider variety and truly lower pricing. Even others today will say (and rightfully so) it is due to online shopping. Whatever the reason, it was a fact that America's romance with the malls was slowly fading away and we had to figure a way to survive since all of the locations were inside malls. (In 2017, the International Council for Shopping Centers puts almost 1/3rd of all malls in serious financial trouble.)

Having worked with people our whole lives we both know that it is virtually impossible to convince someone once they have made up their mind. The key is to change their paradigm of how they view the world. As we analyzed what was happening, we noticed that all of the stores in the mall were starting to suffer, but some more than others. There remained the faithful shoppers who loved to come to the mall, and when they came, they had money in their pockets.

Now, we have all been shopping before, and we know that if we come home without something - anything at all - we feel like we failed! Shopping is no fun unless you buy something – even if it's a cookie! Therefore, we can make this conclusion; **there is no reason to go shopping unless you plan to buy something**. With this being the case, we knew that people would still buy from a mall location. It wasn't just that we had to change the minds of the front-line sales employees, we had to change everything. We had to change the culture.

My mentor at the time, Ron Hill, and myself were the first to recognize this need. Ron sent me out on a mission to change everything about the way we saw our business: from the way we merchandised to the way we sold, to the way we dressed, to the way we advertised. Everything about the company was changing to fit this new belief system that Ron and I were trying to instill. In essence, we were trying changing the retail culture.

The whole thing could be summed up this way. Although we were a company of electronics stores, our competition was not the other electronics stores. It was everyone in the mall. The shoe store, the card store, the bookstore, everyone! When a customer came into the mall, they had money in their pocket, and they would not leave until they left that money with someone, anyone who was good enough to take it.

This explains why clothing stores do so well in malls. You can always rationalize the need for a new blouse, shirt, and pair of pants or shoes. Shoppers love the clothing stores since they are usually their saviors by keeping them from going home feeling like failures. We would even buy something we're not in love with to carry out the door as our trophy – the visible token of the victorious hunter.

What was the one thing that seemed to make all of the difference in where the customer left their money? **An experience. A unique, personalized, inspirational experience.**

Think about this. Let's say that your television went out and you needed a new one. In the electronics business in your area right now, how many stores are there to choose from? Of that number, how many sells LED televisions? All of them. How many of them carry Sony? Again, most likely, all of them. How many of them deliver? All of them. How many of them will service it or have it serviced for you if it breaks? All of them. How many of them have financing? (Are you seeing a pattern here?) And last but not least, how many of them guarantee the lowest price or else they will pay for your child's college tuition? ALL of them! There is even a plethora of stores like Walmart and Target who sell these TVs now.

With this being the case, all an electronics retailer in your town has to do to win your business is to be better than the rest, right? Well, sort of. You see it goes beyond that— way beyond! By the way, the last time you went shopping for a new something (like a television), what was the determining factor? Whether you are a retailer who sells in malls, an outside sales company that sells computer networking services, or a manufacturer of cellular phones, there is one axiom that will always be true for you and your business.

The sting of poor service will last 1,000 times longer than the joy of getting the lowest price.

(We believe that this was originally a verse in Proverbs, but didn't make it in the translation of 1611.)

A few years later, we did a test with a group of managers from a hotel we were consulting with. We wanted them to understand our concept of competition. In the hotel industry, of course, your competition is other hotels. That makes sense. So all you have to do is be better than the other hotels, and you will win. Right? Again, if this is true, why are there so many hotels out there? Granted some of it is due to demand, but many of the hotels sit half empty. There is one exception to this rule – the hotels at Disney World. They proclaim a 97% occupancy rate. Hmm...

Think about your business. Are you the best among your competitors? If so, why are they still in business? There must be something more to it, and there is.

We took the group of hotel managers into a local mall and turned them loose in a Warner Brothers Studio Store with the task of trying to identify what it felt like to do business there. At first, many of the managers were like you, thinking they were there to test the knowledge and skills of the salespeople as a secret shopper. This is only a small part of the **experience** of doing business with someone. We asked them to pay close attention to merchandising, cleanliness, and atmosphere. What did it sound like? How did it make them feel? What were the reactions of the customers shopping to the environment they were in?

Then, we took the group into a Disney Store and had them compare the experience. What was it like? What did it look like? How did it make them feel? The experience was entirely different. But why? Aren't they all competing for the same customer? Go look into these stores and tell me that you don't see the same people shopping in both!

After researching "entertainment stores," we escorted the group into a series of women's skin care stores. (This is significant since 90% of the group was male.) First was Bath and Body Works. This is a small boutique-style store created by The Limited, which sells lotions, bath oils, and skin care products. Again we asked the group to "feel" the store. This time they picked up on the bright colors and beautiful fragrances of the store that they did not experience in the previous stores. Next stop was Origins. The soothing fragrances and "whole body" message were evident in the store design and layout even down to the product names such as "Take the Day Off" makeup remover. Our final stop was in a lesser-known skin care store run on a local level. When the group entered, all the employees were in white smocks, and the fragrances were kept in holders that looked like test tubes. Different environment. Different experience. But they are all going after the same customer—women who care about skin care.

By now you're probably saying to yourself, this is all well and good, but when do we stop the retail lesson and get to the culture change stuff? How about now?

You have decided to instill an experience culture in your company because your company's market share is probably shrinking or your profits or margins are eroding. You have increased turnover and lowered employee morale and productivity. You have recognized the need for a change, but do you recognize why?

There are two points we can draw from the mall experiential completed by this group of hotel managers. First, the experience in the store is directly related to the experience within the company. The company's culture is what shaped the experiences the managers had when they visited. The Warner Brothers Store would like to be like Disney, but what the managers picked up on was that it felt "commercialized" compared to the Disney Store. (Interesting to note, we will not be able to complete this exercise anymore since Warner Brothers stores are all closed.) The group of hoteliers immediately went back and visited their location and began to "feel" it for the first time.

Second, all of them are in competition. The hotel managers were in competition with the mall. How? Because the **experience a customer receives** in the mall will stay with them for a long, long time. It will be the basis for comparison for some time to come. We were not just testing the service of these stores, but their culture.

If you are making this culture shift towards creating a Culturrific! Experience company, then obviously one of your reasons is competition. **But first, your view of competition must change if you are going to be able to compete**.

In today's marketplace, your competition goes way beyond your head-to-head rivals. In the early '90s, when we saw the future of mall retailing competition, we theorized correctly that the money was still there. It was just being grabbed at from more places. It was not our share of the electronics market that mattered; it was our share of the mall dollar. But even this view proves to be short-sighted in today's omnichannel marketplace.

Over the past few years, we have conducted a survey of customers to understand their likelihood to return to a company based on the "experience" they had there. Sometimes we would stand outside a business and talk to customers as they left or we would post on an online survey or even sent surveys to customers via email through various companies.

What was remarkable is that after thousands of submissions and interviews over the last two years, the data has remained the same. Customers no longer want their expectations *met* in retail - they want them **EXCEEDED**! I grew up in a time when **customer service** was all about "satisfying" the customer. The problem with that idea is that for the customer - that is simply not enough anymore.

In today's ultra-competitive marketplace where your competition is not only the other business in town, *and also the other*s online, this research should scare the heck out of you. After all, as a customer, it is very easy to have your expectations met by an online business. You know what you want (at least you think you do). You search for it online. You buy it. They ship it to your home or provide you the service via SaaS. And your expectations are met. Simple - as long as the order is in stock, it ships property, the website works on the first try, etc.

If you want to compete today, you can no longer be in the business of just meeting expectations— **you have to EXCEED them**! There is no other path. This is the reason why so many believe loyalty is dead; because even if you do your job right, the customer still shops around next time. In my book, <u>Signs Sell</u>, co-authored with the great Rick Segel, I coined the term "experience engineering."

To exceed expectations, you must become an "experience engineer.".

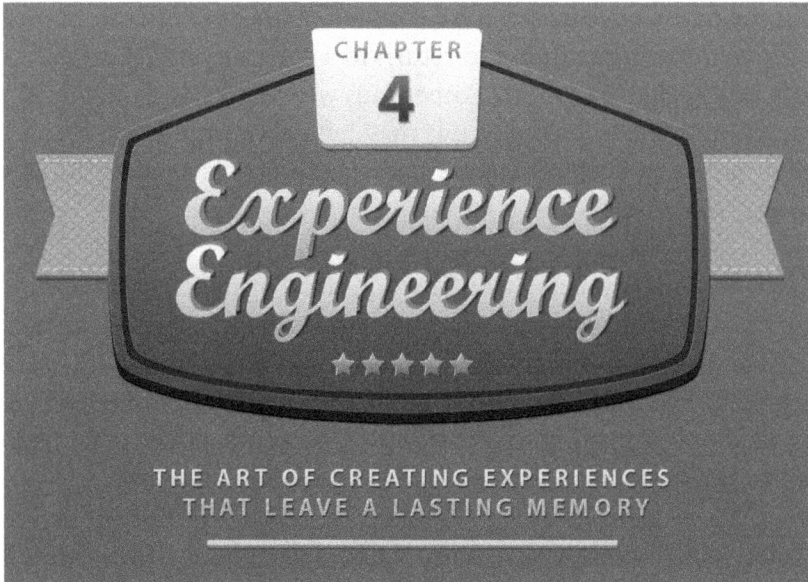

CHAPTER 4

Experience Engineering

★ ★ ★ ★ ★

THE ART OF CREATING EXPERIENCES THAT LEAVE A LASTING MEMORY

In this case, the engineer is *you* the culture change driver — someone who "begins with the end in mind." In other words, start with what the customer experience needs to be (in your case one that *exceeds* expectations) and then create or engineer the processes, policies, training, promotions, building design, website design, signage, and casting (hiring) with the end goal in mind.

Think back to the time when you first started your company. You probably were an engineer, but not an *experience* one. You focused on the brand. But did you consider what the customer experience would be? Probably not. I know I didn't. I was focused on inventory and merchandising. **I was more worried about my logo than I was the customer experience.**

True, none of us ignore the customer in our planning - at least that we will admit - but to be an experienced engineer, you have to *be the customer* and not be the owner. Consider this, when you examine your company, you are thinking like an owner. Your focus is increasing sales or cutting expenses. You view your business through the lens of the P&L statement even if you're a non-profit.

But your customer views your company very differently. They view it through the lens of *experience*. Consider this, is your favorite restaurant the one with the fanciest interior and decor? Is it the one with the most expensive food? Or is it the one you have the best time at? Research proves it's the latter. It's the **experience** you have when dining there that makes it memorable. Some of my favorite places are pretty old and ugly to look at, but the people and the food make it a fun experience. In fact, the outdated interior and the "hole-in-the-wall" atmosphere are part of the appeal. (But I never use the bathroom there.)

Even online businesses are learning the dramatic importance of customer experience. It's why we see so many online-only retailers opening their brick and mortar stores today. Even the ones who said it was taboo to do so like Amazon.com have opened book, convenience, and even grocery stores. They are trying to monitor and gauge the customer experience with products so they can try and translate that online.

I remember sitting on a panel of experts at a retailing conference a few years back, and everyone on the panel was predicting the doom of brick and mortar. In fact, everyone on the panel (except me) said that stores would be gone within 10 years - that the only reason to have a store was to serve as a pickup point for online orders.

While it's true that retailers have used stores for online order pickup as part of a broader omnichannel strategy, the demise of the retail brick and mortar store is not. The reason I gave for my belief that stores would never go away was customer experience. And today, the big guns like Amazon are proving me right. But you didn't have to be a prophet to get this right - you simply need to be a customer yourself.

Who is your competition?

Good question! The answer:

Anyone who provides service!!!!!

Because if you're providing service, then you are providing an *experience*.

If you are reading this book, then you have or want to build a company or organization based on experience. And that means you are focused on both the customer and the employee experience. How do your customers measure your experience? For 99% of the people we consult, they gauge their customer's opinions through "bounce back" or surveys or follow-up phone calls. Many companies get so caught up in this practice that they quantify their data and give scores of their findings. We are not saying this is a bad practice, just that it falls short. If you only measure yourself against yourself, then all you are really saying is "you are better than you" or "worse than you" whichever the case is. (Now that is a scary thought.)

Some companies have gone beyond the traditional "how did we do" types of surveys to include questions to measure them against their competition. They look to see if their service stacks up against their head-to-head competitors. We call these head-to-head competitors the **visible** competition. We applaud these companies for getting to the next step, but they are like we were back at the electronics retailer – still one step short.

Think about your quest for service. One of the first questions we ask people who are wanting to make their culture a strong experience culture is "Who would you say provides the best customer experience?" Their answers are probably similar to yours. Responses like Disney, Nordstrom, Southwest Airlines, Zappos, REI, and others come to mind. The next question we ask is a little unexpected. "Who would you say provides the worst experience?" Here the responses start to become more random. They tend to be related to the area of the country the person is from. But there is never any hesitation with this question when people respond. The answers come just as quickly when we discuss bad service as they do when we discuss great service.

Interestingly though, they are never comparison/ contrast responses. For example, if they said Nordstrom for great experience, they didn't say another department store for the poor experience. They might say Charter cable or Sprint. Companies that are not in direct competition at all.

Answer these two questions for yourself.

Who comes to your mind when you think of great experience?

Why?

The second question is more important than the first. The reason you think this place is so wonderful is what counts. Now answer these two questions.

Who comes to mind when you think of poor experience?

Why?

Again, the second question is the most important. Here's why: Whenever we have a tremendous experience, it sticks in our minds forever. We share this experience with our friends adding more glamour to the story each time. **This experience is important because it becomes more than just a one-time event – it becomes the benchmark by which you measure all other services you receive**. We even use these experiences to compare with others. We have phrases in our language like "It was just like being at Disney!" or more generic statements like "It was like eating at a five-star restaurant."

Apply this idea to the poor experiences you noted. Don't you do the same thing? Poor service has phrases in our language as well. "It was like getting my driver's license renewed!" or "It was like buying a used car." Or "It was like going to the dentist!" This last one is amazing since the dentist gets compared when they are in a totally different industry. We never think of dentists as service providers, do we?

Think about all the different companies you do service with on a daily basis. Whether it's on the phone or in person, the impression that stays with you is the same. Zappos has an excellent reputation for providing superior service, yet you probably have never seen a Zappos employee in your life. But, if you ever bought from them, you remember the experience.

In a society as fickle as ours is today, service is the price of entry into the race. At one time it was quality, after that it was price, then it was great service, but today and forever it is an experience. **Your competition has grown beyond the visible to the unvisible**. "Unvisible" is not a real word, but it is the phrase I coined to describe this idea.

Yes, I have exercised some creative license here in creating a new word, I know. The word typically used here is invisible. But if you look up the definition of invisible in the American Heritage Dictionary, you will find "something that cannot be seen." This doesn't fit our purposes here. It's not that we cannot see this new form of competition; we just haven't in the past. But you can see it if we look for it.

Before you move forward, you must first:

Define your visible and unvisible competition.

Who are they? Why are they on the list? Make a comprehensive list of what makes them your competition. Then make a comprehensive list of what attributes they have that earned them a spot on your list. This exercise will be very important for the rest of the stops in this book. Make sure that your training and development department incorporates this philosophy in their culture training classes. In fact, do this exercise you are about to do part of every new employee's first day of training. This will help them understand your broader definition of **experience**.

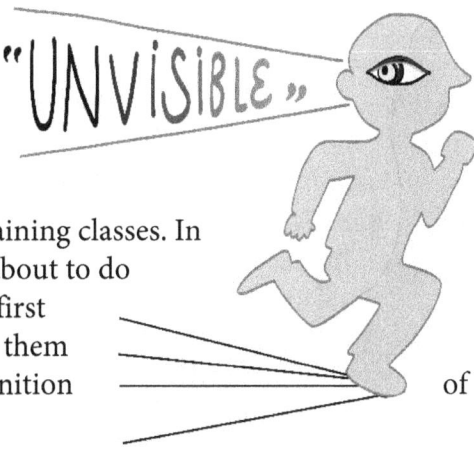

Take your time with this and be careful not to hurry through it. We cannot emphasize enough the impact of this step and the understanding of the two types of competition. (By the way, don't bother with the poor experience list, unless of course, that is what you want to become!)

We live in the ATM generation. You may have heard the more common Millennial or Generation Z stories, but we like to think of what is going on as the ATM generation. People living and buying today have most likely spent their lives using ATMs or a mobile app instead of tellers, and streaming movies instead of reading. Fast food drive-thrus were a perfect idea at the time, after all, the process of buying a burger that used to take ten minutes now only takes four. But today people want more. So when you are in the drive-thru now, if you sit more than two minutes, you start to honk the horn in disgust.

The idea is so commonplace that something different is now the quest. My parents will not own an ATM card even though their bank offers them. They do not trust them and never will. I find this humorous; but then again, I can't recall the last time I was in a bank. With direct deposit and my bank's app, my life is taken care of electronically. The number of typing errors made in the last paragraph alone that have been automatically corrected is the very reason most typewriters were destroyed decades ago.

This is the customer of today. **Things that seem wonderful today will be commonplace tomorrow, and the cycle will continue for infinity**. It has always been this way. If you have ever read the Bible, you will recall an angel named Lucifer. Lucifer was the #2 guy in Heaven. This would be the ultimate spot to be one would think – Heaven. But Lucifer started taking it all for granted and set out to be God's competitor and tried to build a new and improved Heaven where he was the ruler.

Again, great just wasn't good enough. Today, fast food drive-thrus aren't good enough. McDonald's delivers through Uber. Music videos aren't good enough anymore. We need virtual reality. The world of the Internet has redefined our lives more dramatically than anyone could have predicted. We want more. Feed our senses and make doing business with you an experience. This is the cry of the customer.

Know thy customer as you know thyself.

This is the 11th commandment. Do not confuse this by thinking it means your customers will want what you want. Not at all. This is what is being said in many boardrooms and front line staff meetings around the country. Oh sure, we preach do unto others, but what if what the others want is different than what we want? My parents don't want an ATM card. So why do it unto them?
Because ATMs make the bank's life so much better? For what they charge to use the ATM, it probably does.

The 11th commandment is the birth of the new platinum rule as Og Mandino calls it. If you want to be successful today, "Do unto others as you would have them do unto you" is not enough. The new rule is

"Treat others the way they want to be treated."

That's right, the way they want to be treated. Not you. Your culture and your competition are directly tied to your customer. That is the basis for this book. And in today's digitally connected world, this axiom has never been truer. If I don't like how you treat me in person, I will just get it on-line! But of course, as fast as the ".comers" rose, many have fallen even harder. They built fabulous cultures to work within, but not fabulous cultures to buy from. They violated the Experience Formula rules. Ah, but I am getting ahead of myself.

At the beginning of Chapter One, I started with a story. There is another reason I told you about Ron Hill. This was my first experience with a culture change. One that ended fatally. Ron and some of the key people left to start a new company before the new culture had been instilled and because the "programming" of the current culture was so strong; we were almost powerless against it.

We were not the President or the CEO. And if there is one lesson we have learned about culture change it's this – **no matter how great a plan or how hard you try, if the TOP is not on board your bus, then you will be driving in circles**. We could preach for hours the importance of top-down commitment, but you already know this. It bears being stated, though, that unless this is truly the case, DON'T EVEN BOTHER! The culture of the executives in this company was so strong (after all they had been doing this for 25 years!) that it would rather die than change. We find this to be common.

Why? Look at the electronics mall store story we were telling. Guess where this retailer is today? That's right, retail heaven. They are no more. Top management fought the culture change and caused it to stall and eventually fail. The failure of the culture change resulted in the failure of the company, and eventually, all of its stores were closed.

Take a look at the companies you admire most and see which ones you'll find on the top ten list of companies to work for in America. You will undoubtedly find a CEO who's passionate about how the company takes care of its customers and employees – **experience.**

Certainly, I am not telling you this to boost your confidence in this book. Other more positive experiences have worked, I can and will share as well. But it was only through the failure at our first attempt (well, the first couple of attempts) that I really started to dig deep into the understanding of what makes a culture work. I had to see what goes wrong to know how to make it right. That first experiences taught me a great deal but, most importantly, it taught me about **the bus**.

What bus? The culture change bus. As you start this process, it is like loading everyone on a bus and stepping on the gas. You are all heading in the same direction together. But even though everyone is on the bus and you are all physically together, there will be many times when the emotions will run high, and the passengers will start to make you crazy. You'll turn to the driver of the bus and swear that it's Sandra Bullock and you are on the bus from the movie "Speed!"

This analogy is more than just humor. It's frighteningly accurate! There will be times during the next months and for some years that will seem like the bus is moving out of control. But remember one thing; if you drop below 55, you're dead. The minute you let the momentum for your culture change drop, the stalling of it is next. And in our times, there have been only a couple of culture change initiatives to succeed once they have stalled.

You must commit yourself right now to this promise. No matter how grim it looks, you are driving the bus. If you turn it over to someone else, you end up just a speed bump on the highway of change and the only thing you will have left to remind you will be the tread marks on your back as the bus speeds on down the road or off a cliff, depending on the new driver.

You might think the quote at the beginning of this chapter was quite odd: **"Culture change is not for the weak of heart."** Well, every good attraction at an amusement park has a sign that lists all sorts of warnings and disclaimers that you must read and agree to before going on the ride. Sometimes you have to wonder if they are there to simply enhance the experience or if they are real concerns.

The thoughts in this book were put here to help you take the right steps in trying to create your new **experience culture**. There are no restrictions or height limitations for this ride, except one—*You* must drive the bus. So, let's work on getting you your driver's license.

License to Drive

There are a lot of people on the culture change road driving under the influence – the influence that they know what they are doing. These drivers give culture change a bad name. Unfortunately, there is no law against DUI culture change.

So, you want to be a card-carrying member of the culture change elite? Well, before we can grant you an official driver's license, you must first have a lesson on corporate culture. At no point do 'I intend to make you experts on the subject of culture, but for you to understand the importance of many of the points of this book, we need to build the foundation and framework.

But first, is it really worth it for you to invest your time and the company's money in trying to create an experience culture within your organization? Take the test on the next page.

y×e×s=$$

Take this test....

Related in a %, how much of the workday is lost in your company due to cultural issues? These issues include low productivity, complaining, gossiping, "passing the buck", etc.

$$y = \rule{3cm}{0.4pt}$$

What is the average (individual) annual salary in your company?

$$e = \rule{3cm}{0.4pt}$$

How many employees are there in your company?

$$S = \rule{3cm}{0.4pt}$$

Complete the following equation.

$$y \times e \times S = \rule{5cm}{0.4pt}$$

(The answer is YES!!)

If you are like most, the value given to Y varies from 5 to 25% depending on whom you're asking. If a company has 3,000 employees (S) in it and the average salary is $30,000 annually (E) and the amount of time wasted is 10% (Y), then the amount of money lost to your culture is $9,000,000. Do we have your attention yet? Would it be all right with your CEO and stakeholders if you added an extra nine million to the bottom line next year?

Okay, but I'm not a 3,000 person company, you might be saying. I have small landscaping service. I have 12 employees, not 3,000. Okay, if this is you - do me a favor - run the math. No matter what size your company or organization is, you will find that culture costs money. Period.

What is the secret to capturing back this money? Your company's corporate culture. I am not saying that you will recover all of this money from reading this book. You will be investing quite a bit of money to get there. But I do think you will save enough money to pay for the investment of this book. So we are even. But, take heart. You'll recover more than just the price of this book!

Several years ago, I sat in the office of Howard Shultz of Starbucks. We were doing some research for a project, and I was on the team. All that to say, it was not my meeting, but I got to be there.

One of the questions the lead of the project asked Howard was "what it your biggest fear as a CEO?" His response, "being able to keep Starbucks' culture alive and well in the stores as they expand." His concern was that the more stores they added (and the faster they expanded), the harder it would be to preserve Starbucks' culture and unique coffee buying experience he had cultivated in the first stores.

In 2000, a few years after the interview, Howard stepped away as CEO and Starbucks started to lose its luster. Some say they expanded too fast. Others say they it was because they entered into new and different products and got away from its core. Howard would say it was because of the dilution of the culture. The **experience** in the Starbucks stores opening at that time he was away was far different than the ones when he was CEO. The focus was on efficiency and operational excellence and not on customer experience.

Howard came back in 2008 and dedicated his life to restoring the Starbucks brand by reviving its unique culture. He even chronicled his journey in a book <u>Onward: How Starbucks Fought for Its Life Without Losing Its Soul.</u> In 2017, Howard finally felt he had everything in place – specifically the right people on the bus – to be able to step down from CEO. But he spent 9 years grooming the right people and putting them in the right places before he did.

What is the definition of culture?

Here is where we dig out our friend Mr. American Heritage Dictionary to help us. (Yes the actual book, not online.) This friend will be very useful to us throughout this book. There are multiple definitions of this word, as there are for all words in the dictionary. The interesting thing about each is how the latter ones grow from the former. See what we mean.

Culture:
1. The behavior patterns, arts, beliefs, institutions, and all other products of human work and thought expressed in a particular community or period.
2. Intellectual and artistic activity and the works produced.
3. Development of the intellect through training or education.

NOTE: These definitions are for the word culture, not for the term corporate culture. Is there any difference? None whatsoever. In definition 1, you replace the word community or period with company and Walla! In definition 2, the works produced (results) of a company. And in definition 3, the intellectual capital of a company. We are especially fond of definition 3. It holds the key to corporate culture and more importantly to corporate culture change.

We could spend the rest of this book discussing the intricacies of culture in more detail, but one of the Top 10 reasons you bought this book is because it wasn't going to be a Harvard edition. The brief description above is all you need to know. However, to effectively change a culture, as in your case of building an **experience culture**, there is a little more you need to know. The people in your company right now are the ones you want to become more service oriented. What's the secret before you go any further? You must involve the whole employee in an experience culture.

John Parker Stewart, in his work <u>Team of Champions</u>, relates it this way; "**with a paycheck, you earn the hands and feet of the employee. But for them to perform at a high service (experience) level, you must capture their hearts and their heads.**" Truer words have never been spoken. How many times have you said to yourself after a poor performance, "My heart just wasn't in it?" If you are like everyone else in the world, way too many. This supports Stewart's and my point. You must have the hearts and heads of your employees if you ever expect them to perform like a Culturrific! experience team. And you need that team to provide an experience that **exceeds your customers' expectations every time**.

It is a fact that a great percentage of your current employees come to work simply looking for the easiest route to a paycheck. These employees look to give the least amount of effort possible to get by. Truly this is their motto— "to get something for nothing."

A group of scientists were performing an experiment with mice. (I know this is a shock and hard to believe, but it's true.) They took a mouse and dropped him into a beaker full of water to see how he would react. The little mouse swam furiously trying to keep its head above the water so it could breathe. Eventually, the mouse's legs tired and he stopped struggling and simply sank to the bottom. The scientists pulled the mouse out of the water, dried him off and put him back in his cage.

The next day, they took the same mouse and placed him in the beaker of water again. This time the mouse swam, and he swam trying to keep his head above water, but not as long this time as he did yesterday before he finally gave up and sank to the bottom. It's now the third day – same mouse, same scientists, and a same beaker of water. They dropped the mouse into the water and guess what happened? The mouse sank straight to the bottom. He had learned that there was no reason to go through the entire struggle and pain of trying to keep his head above water. In essence, the mouse had learned that if he would just sink to the bottom, they would take him out, dry him off and it would all be over. **If it takes a mouse three days to learn he can get something for nothing, how long does it take people?**

Let's face it. You have a workforce with lots of hands-and-feet people who are looking to get something for nothing. These are not the experience providers you need. However, in most cases, it's simply because no one has ever tried to touch their hearts and heads. They have spent their adult lives "getting by" looking for the path of least resistance. But what about yourself? Have you always been a go-getter? Or is there some point in your life when someone got to your heart and head that made the difference in who you are today? Take a couple of minutes to think about this point really. You could, in fact, be that person for the employees in your company.

We are not advocating that you will have to fire all of your employees and start over. This is a ludicrous proposition (although tried by some.) The stops in this book are designed with the above philosophy. Every action you take from now on will look to capture the hearts and heads of your employees so that they can make a difference in the lives of your customers.

A corporate culture is a living, breathing part of your company.

There was a scorpion that happened onto a river on his journey home. Being a scorpion, he couldn't swim across the river, so he needed help. The scorpion spotted a frog sitting on the edge of the river. He approached the frog and asked him to let him climb on the frog's back and ride across the river.

"I can't do that," said the frog. "You are a scorpion! You will sting me!" "I won't sting you, "said the scorpion. "If I did, I would only be hurting myself because if you drown, so do I!" The frog thought it over and finally agreed. The scorpion climbed onto the frog's back, and they started across the river. Halfway across, the frog felt a painful sensation in his back. The scorpion had stung him. "I can't believe you did that," said the frog. "Why? Why did you do it?" asked the frog going down for the last time. "Because I am a scorpion," he replied, "and that's what scorpions do."

What is the moral of this story? You must accept the fact that your corporate culture is a real entity, not just a buzzword. The definitions given above can be cold and well, "dictionary-like." Once you have accepted the fact that your **corporate culture is a living, breathing thing**, then and only then can you initialize true change in your organization. You must realize that your culture has a heart and a head and that you must deal with both. The scorpion in this story is your current culture. Your warning is not to claim victory with your experience culture change initiative too early. On the outside, the scorpion convinced the frog (management in this scenario) that he was all for change and would not practice old habits. But the further across the river (culture change) the frog and scorpion got, the harder it was for the scorpion to accept this "head" decision and he started to follow his heart and stung the frog.

You will get stung continually unless you accept the fact that true culture change is much deeper than a few rules and policy changes. It goes so much further than dressing casual and calling everyone by his or her first names. You must get to the heart of the culture and change its identity.

cul|ture (kul'cher), n., v.,-tured, -tur|ing. —n. development of the intellect through training or education.

What is the identity of a culture?

For years, business strategists and consultants have preached about the power of image or brand in the marketplace. What image does your company have? What image of your company do your employees have? What do four out of five dentists say about your company? All of these are very important statistics for knowing what people think. **But the measure of a company's culture is not made by its image but through its identity.**

The American Heritage Dictionary defines an image as "the concept or character projected to the public." This wordy definition is trying to say "how others see your company." We can fool great numbers of people with positive images. The advertising magicians cast wonderful spells on the imaginations of the public and convince them that all is well in your kingdom.

Image even has a place internally. Through your internal marketing (sometimes better known as spin), you can convince your employees that all is well even when it isn't. But this fact you cannot dispute – the identity of your culture will always win out over your image.

Identity is "who your company really is" – the values and beliefs of the culture. You must change your culture's identity, not its image. This is a fatal error that befalls many companies embarking on culture change.

Identity is the heart of your culture. The image is the head (mind) of your culture. It's much easier to change your mind than it is to change your heart.

For example, if your company has been a hierarchical, policy-driven organization in the past and now you want to change it to being service or customer oriented focused on experience, what you have to change is your company's identity. You must reshape who you are and what you stand for otherwise, the old identity will kick in, and you and your customers will be stung.

The best example of this would be the AT&T Company breakup into the baby Bells. AT&T had long been the ruler of the telecommunications kingdom. They made the rules, and if you wanted to talk on a phone, you had to follow them. Would you like new phone service? We will get it to you when we feel like it. Do you have a question about your bill? We will be happy to answer it when we are good and ready but, of course, you understand that you will have to be transferred several times before you get your answer.

The big awakening came when AT&T was broken up into the "baby Bells, " and they had to compete for the same exact customer they had been serving for many years. Their culture had to change for them to survive. Bell Atlantic is regularly touted as the one who was first and best at establishing a service culture.

The modern day equivalent of the telephone shake-up is satellite television. Several years ago, RCA changed the way we view television when they started to sell Direct Broadcast satellite dishes that were no larger than 17" and gave you all the beautiful digital pictures you could ever want. The best part was that you got all of this for the same price your cable operator was charging you for the sorry 20 channel lineup they were providing.

To make matters worse for the cable companies, along came another player – DISH Network. The DISH Network system used the same principle as RCA, but they did not require you to purchase any equipment, just the service. That would be like your cable company not requiring you to have a converter box to use their service.

What resulted was that people got:
- better sound quality (digital v. analog)
- better picture quality (digital again)
- better variety (up to four movie channels included in the base price each month)
- less hassle

The interesting thing to watch is how the cable companies respond to this new threat to their market share. One thing is for sure; they have always had the operational approach to business, not the customer approach. They will not win over anyone with their current cultures. (this might be why AT&T bought DirecTV – a cable provider bought a satellite provider rather than adapt.

These companies, like many, have reached what Andrew Grove, former CEO of Intel who passed recently, calls in his book, <u>Only the Paranoid Survive</u>, a "strategic inflection point." Grove's strategic inflection point (SIP) philosophy can be closely related to culture change. A company's SIP is when they realize the competition or the customer has changed the rules and it's time to change. **The corporate culture is the first place to start.**

In the first version of this book, I predicted the demise of the video rental world dominated by Blockbuster and Hollywood Entertainment. Streaming services like Vudu and Netflix and kiosk-based rentals like Redbox meant that the experience for the customer was enhanced. It's easier than ordering a pizza. And with streaming services, you don't even have to get out of your pajamas.

The point of the story was that I believed these companies would not adjust their thinking because I had interacted with their executives and experienced their cultures. Changing their business model would have been like turning an aircraft carrier around in the Mississippi River. And sadly, they didn't evolve, and their cultures drove them out of business. The experience the customer received wasn't enough to compete

The Five Key Elements of an Experience Culture

What are the key elements of an experience culture? Well, there are five to be exact. These five represent the heart of your culture and are where you must begin your change. The first two represent the visible parts of your culture – those things that your employees can easily see. The last two represent the "unvisible" part of your culture, and the middle one is on the fringe since it has elements from both sides.

You will recall that our definition of "unvisible" was **"things that are not seen but are there if we look for them."** Invisible means you could never see them. Unvisible means you must look for them because they can be seen if you try hard enough; they are there. In the world of culture change, it is the "unvisible" that will crash your bus more than the visible. As we like to say, Everything Speaks (that's what the network guys call a tease for an upcoming chapter).

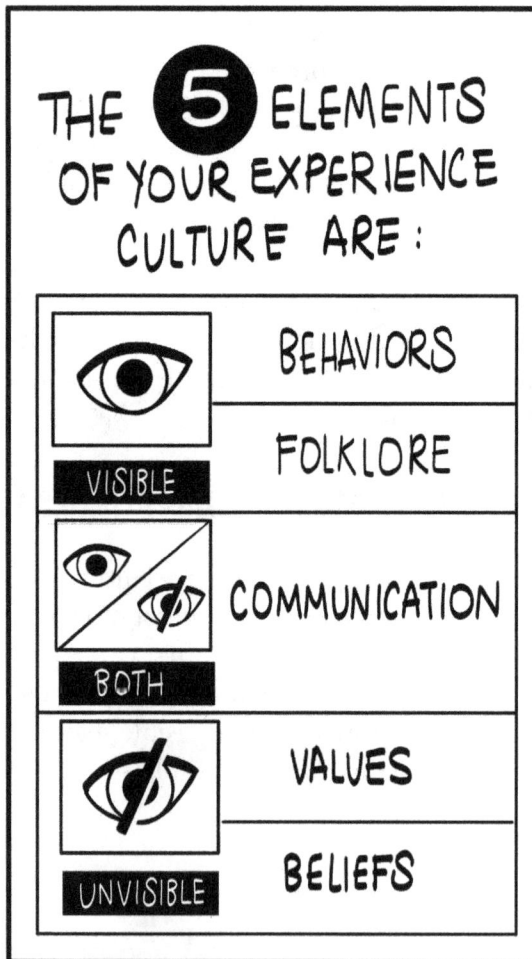

THE **5** ELEMENTS
OF YOUR EXPERIENCE
CULTURE ARE:

VISIBLE	BEHAVIORS
	FOLKLORE
BOTH	COMMUNICATION
UNVISIBLE	VALUES
	BELIEFS

Behaviors

This one is pretty simple to figure out. How do your people behave on a daily basis in their roles? What we have on paper and what we do are two various things. As we all know, actions do speak louder than words. **But in culture change, it is not only the verbal but the non-verbal behavior as well.**

How do your people react to a crisis? How do they celebrate? Do they celebrate? Do they work as a team? Do their behaviors value the customer experience? Do their behaviors value the employee experience? Do their behaviors value the stakeholder experience? The behaviors in your culture are fairly easy to see and decipher although sometimes you will have to decode some of the behaviors.

Behaviors also manifest themselves in our dress, the quality, and timeliness of our work, even the amount of time we take for lunch. People react differently to different situations. You probably have a much different behavior set for when you attend church than when you are at a friend's house. Or compare the way you act at work versus the way you act at home. How do they differ? Your behaviors are congruent with the culture or situation you find yourself in at the given time. Culture does not make you schizophrenic, but it does affect the way you behave.

When I was working as a lead consultant for a Fortune 50 tech client in Texas, I experienced a corporate culture like none other. The amount of productivity and work churned out by the employees was remarkable. The problem was work-life balance non-existent. It was an extremely stressful place to work. In fact, if you didn't have two meetings scheduled for the same time you were not working. The behaviors of the employees celebrated the overworked and criticized the person who simply had one meeting at a time.

Earlier I mentioned that the non-verbal behaviors are just as important in culture as the verbal. This is especially true in an experience culture. How many times have you been waited on by a salesperson or service provider and could tell from his or her non-verbal behavior that they didn't want to be at work that day?

I was checking out at a Lowe's Home Improvement store one time, and the lead cashier came over and spoke to the cashier waiting on me. Whatever the conversation, the cashier was not happy. She turned around and began ringing up my items. The entire time she was whispering to herself and shaking her head. You could tell she was upset and it affected her ability to provide a remarkable customer experience. In fact, I had one item under the cart on the rack, and she said to me, "well, are you going to pull that out or not?" Nice.

Folklore

This is where the traditions of your culture come to life. We are story-formed people. Even before we could write, we would tell stories. Folklore got its name from the stories people used to tell around the campfires at night. The elders would gather the village together and tell them of their history – their origin. Where did they come from? Why are they where they are today? What do they stand for? Who were the heroes of their people? It was the only way the information was passed on. There were no books or digital cameras, and it was centuries before Al Gore invented the Internet.

Just like the stories of the elders, your company has its folklore as well. It is told every day in the break room, at lunch, on the phone to customers, in the interview to prospective employees and on and on. See if any of these sound familiar.

- "Be careful, Brayden did that one time, and it cost him his job!"
- "Our founder built this company working 16 hours a day; I think an hour of overtime won't kill you!"
- "You know when I was in your position; we didn't have computers."
- "You know when I was your age, we had to walk to school in 12 feet of snow!" (Oops, sorry, flashbacks growing up in Indiana there.)

And my all-time favorite -

- "Well, that's just the way we have always done it around here."

What are your traditions? Don't know? Try some of the ones above. Is there an urgency addiction in your culture? This was Stephen Covey's (7 Habits of Highly Effective People) term for people who actually loved the overworked life. You know the type; they always eat lunch at their desk with a sandwich in one hand typing email with the other.

Does everyone complain all the time because they are always putting out fires? Is everything last minute? Who are the heroes of the workplace? Are they the ones with the highest sales or the best customer experience? This one is tough because your executive's or manager's heroes and your hourly people's heroes are probably two very different people.

Do you want to know why people don't know who the heroes are in their company? Because it's not part of the process! It is never discussed in training. It is never discussed in meetings. There are no bi-monthly celebrations to brag on your people. As a matter of fact, in most companies, the tradition is to get together once a year for the obligatory Christmas party, and that's it. Then the employee has to endure a speech on how valuable he is to the company. Do you think they feel valuable if this is the case?

When I use the term folklore, I am describing a way to tell your company history and background that relates to the hearts and heads of your people. If you show the PowerPoint slides or the 80' x 100' color, glossy portrait of the founder to everyone as part of their indoctrination into your company, you are asking them to give you their hands and feet. You must reach them – relate to them! Tell them stories! Stories like your grandparents did, or the elders did in early civilizations. Instead of saying, "The Grandiose Company was founded in 1943 by Ben. He got the idea from people watching at the fair."

Try this on for size instead. "It's July 17, 1943, and Ben is standing on the stairwell overlooking the midway at the county fair in Everett, Texas. He had been noticing the way people were continually fanning themselves with their tickets while they wait in line. And then suddenly it hits him. What if you could make a fan that was small enough to fit in the palm of your hand? A woman could carry it in her purse, and it would be battery operated. Excitedly, Ted ran back to the office and started drawing up the plans for the Hand Fan, our first ever product at Grandiose. And that tradition of the invention is what drives us still today."

Notice the difference. It was like you were hearing a story about someone instead of hearing a lecture. Do you know the other reason people loved to sit around the fire and listen to the folklore? It made them feel like they were part of something. Everyone wants to feel like they are part of something. In a later chapter, I will talk about the fact that people draw the majority of their self-esteem from their job. Why? Because they want to belong to something – something special.

How do you tell your employees about your traditions or your folklore? What stories do you share? We live in the ATM generation; they need to be entertained. Walt Disney once said, "**I would much rather entertain someone in hopes of training them than to train someone in hopes of entertaining them**." Walt had the right formula and so can you.

48

What traditions do you want to be present in your experience culture? Celebration? Recognition? Integrity? Care? Passion? Teamwork? Risk? Are your people afraid to step out and take a chance? If so, it's an example of the tradition in your company. And the traditions are carried from one department to the next from one employee to the net from one generation to the next through stories – through folklore.

Communication

Communication within your experience culture is not about reaching an agreement with your employees; **it's about reaching an understanding with your employees**. The communication element of your culture can be divided into three parts. They are the:

1. Vocabulary of your company
2. Language of your company
3. Internal and external communication of your company

1. Vocabulary of your company

Your culture's vocabulary is the terms you are adopting to create uniqueness among your experience team. This is a very important step because it is an obvious sign that things are different. Perhaps you want to call everyone cast members like Disney or Team Members like Target Stores. Whatever you decide, it must be based on your culture's theme.

A culture's theme is the metaphor you are using to describe the behaviors, values, communication, folklore, and beliefs of your culture. This is the trendy part of culture change that is not necessary but highly recommended for the visible reason listed above. Be careful not to go too crazy with this step. Use terms that your people can understand and will accept. Also, if you are "theming" your culture, there is no need to use the terms from the metaphor exactly.

For example, in one culture change for a conference center we worked with, they selected a movie studio theme. The term for coffee breaks and snack foods in the movie industry is "craft services." We elected not to use this term because everyone thought they were getting Popsicle sticks and Elmer's glue on the tray instead of coffee. You can see that the confusion this caused was negative and detracted from the customer experience. However, it's important to note that much of your new vocabulary will be confusing at first. This will take time. **DO NOT make the mistake of starting out with one term and changing it to another**. This is the easiest road to failure.

2. Language of your company

The language of your culture relates to the way you talk to one another. Especially in the computer or SaaS industries, acronyms and slang terms are prevalent. People quickly forget that the rest of the world has no idea what they are talking about. Things seem so simple to us, but they are very complicated to others. Be careful to make sure that your terms or slang are eliminated. How we talk to each other is how we will talk to the customer.

When I used to sell electronics, there was always a pitch at the end for an extended warranty. We had a one-year, two-year or three-year plan available for each product. Around the water cooler, we referred to the three-year deal as the "full boat" warranty. This was our little way of saying we got the maximum money from the customer. It was no big deal until one day when I overheard one of the new guys saying to the customer, "Well, my recommendation is that you get the full boat warranty!" Isolated incident? Hardly. Eliminate the short-cut terms in your culture that can confuse and destroy your service excellence and give the customer a poor experience.

Another way to look at the language of your culture is to check for colorful adjectives when people speak. **Swearing shows a lack of professionalism and respect** and, just as slang terms can make their way into conversations with customers, so too often do these four-letter words.

Also, the volume at which your language is communicated tells a lot about your culture. Too many people practice the deaf principle today. You know this one. It's when we speak louder to someone who is deaf as if that will help him or her understand you. Many managers think that the only way to emphasize their point is through yelling. There is never a need to raise your voice in an experience culture unless you are cheering. In fact, if you do, the "experience" is a bad one.

3. Internal and external communication of your company

One of the first stops on your culture change journey is to define your company's product. The challenge will be when it comes to communication of the product. How do you communicate it to the public? The biggest mistake a company can make is when they try to wear two faces – one for the public (external) and one for the employee (internal). For example, at DisneyWorld, employees are called cast members. This is what they call them to anyone they talk to. They do not apologize for their culture. They may have to explain themselves a few times a day when communicating with the outside world, but that's okay. It reaffirms the culture's identity over and over.

This was a lesson we learned the hard way. One of our first real culture change projects was to open a new retail concept with existing people from an old culture. We gave them Disney and, in so doing, used the term guest instead of the customer. We went about creating this culture and were derailed when the upper, upper management said, "You cannot put the word guest on a sign! It will confuse everyone!"

So, we were required to use the word customer everywhere it was to be external, but they were kind enough to let us place a guest on all of our internal communication! The result was utter confusion. The cast members (employees) were so confused because all their training taught them, guest, yet when they entered the "real world" it still said customer. We spent 80-100 hours training every new employee before we opened the doors to each location. It was our version of brainwashing, and it worked marvelously until internal became in conflict with external. (By the way, the signs eventually changed to guest.)

Another company we worked with wanted to convey their newly defined product of "style" (more on "product" to come) to the world. So we renamed the sales associates Style Consultants. At first, as is usually the case, the people thought it hokey and resisted. But through time, a sense of pride and the true meaning of the word "style" evolved in this culture. People shopped at this store because the people are called Style Consultants. And the quality of employee attracted increased as well. This company effectively "programmed" style in the position and it worked magically.

Programming is what determines your culture, and there is no greater form of programming than how your employees see you interact with the public. If you tell your employees that in your new experience culture they will no longer be called employees, but will be called team members, then you better carry that all the way through if you expect it to stick.

What do we mean by all the way through? **EVERYTHING better reflect this new term.**

This is where you will struggle the most. If in your new experience culture, you decide to change parts one and two – the vocabulary and language, then you will have the hardest sell with your upper management and your legal department. They will not change their vocabulary so quickly. They are set in their ways, and besides, what does saying team member have to do with them? Once again, Everything Speaks (you know, eventually I need to define this term for you).

OUT	IN
EMPLOYEE	TEAM
HANDBOOK	MEMBER GUIDE
BREAKROOM	LOCKER ROOM
DISCOUNT	MEMBER DISCOUNT
PARKING	MEMBER PARKING
OF THE MONTH	MVP
PERSONNEL	CASTING

The last important note on communication is when and how. How often do you get the whole company together to celebrate accomplishments and discuss the business? Understandably, if you are a business with 300 locations nationwide this is difficult to do, but how often do each of the locations get together? You should plan to have a meeting for all of your employees twice a month.

In this meeting be prepared to discuss the following in no particular order:

- Financial data (How well are we doing. Be honest! In a later chapter on the younger generations you will see why.)
- Goals (Where we are in relation to our goals. Talk about company goals here, not departmental. Keep them focused on the big picture.)
- Folklore (Continue to tell the stories of your company.)
- Celebrate (Give out awards and recognition for those who deserve.)
- Announcements (What's coming up in the future.)
- State of the Union (What is the company up to?)

If you are trying to build an **experience culture**, then you better make sure the front-line employees are involved in these meetings. You are trying to get your employees to be of service to each other as well as the customer. Your people see your face often enough. **Let the peers tell the stories and give out the information.** This will communicate a very strong message for you. Newsletters and social media are great communication tools. We will give you more hints on how to use these in the chapters on "Awards and Recognition" and "Culture Council."

Values

The first element of the unvisible category of culture is the values of your culture. Values provide a sense of common direction among the employees of the company. This is the start of your company's identity. The values you adopt will determine the behaviors you witness every day from your employees. What does your culture value and hold dear? Is it hard work? Is it precision? Is it getting the deal whatever the cost? Is it family? Is it the customer experience?

Every company we talk with preaches the customer as one of its values, but usually, this isn't in place in the culture. I will deal with the values of your experience culture in more detail in another chapter, but for now, it is enough to know that the word value in this context is exactly as you thought – a principle, standard or quality thought of as worthwhile.

Remember our tech client from the Behaviors section? This culture uniquely valued time. Checking your email at midnight was considered proper work style and often expected by managers. Earns you props with your boss, though definitely not a favorite activity of your spouse.

You will come to understand that what your culture values will ultimately determine the behaviors of your employees. And you also need to know that the reason we put values in the unvisible category is that in my experiences what the owners think the values of the company are and what they employees actually value are very different.

Beliefs

Whereas values are words that relate worth to us in our culture, beliefs are the principles or strongly-held convictions of the culture. If you are paying close attention to each of these explanations, you are starting to see a pattern or "cycle" develop. This is known as **the culture cycle**. The culture cycle delivers the theory that your beliefs (since they are "strongly-held convictions") come before your values (which show "worth or regard for something") and the behaviors of your culture are born from the beliefs and values.

Beliefs actually go deeper than values since they are formed before the values (this will make more sense in the Culture Cycle discussion) because what you believe about something determines its value to you. For example, if you believe in God, then your value system reflects a creator and deity you worship or serve. If you are an atheist, then your value system will be different. You will draw more of your values from human sources (books, the internet, etc.) versus the Bible.

All five experience culture elements will intertwine with each other. They are interdependent. You cannot attack one of the five and expect any level of success. The culture cycle is an important fundamental yet to come in your culture change training. In the meantime, let's continue our discussions on the definition and makeup of corporate culture.

The Two Sides of an Experience Culture

There are two sides to your culture – the people side and the process side. Each has an equal weight yet one side of the culture will get more focus, and one side will get ignored, depending on who is leading your culture change and what type of company you have now.

People

How do you define each part? First the people side. This is the human side of your culture where feelings, emotions, and self-esteem are kept. As we go further in this book together, we will talk more about the people side. As a matter of fact, the majority of this book is about the people side! This is the hardest side to deal with in a culture change. It is the part with the most resistance to change and the least amount of visible gain.

To build the people side of your culture, I usually start with this activity. Once a month, the management staff gets together for a two-hour lunch off site. They get to enjoy themselves because there is only one rule – **YOU CANNOT TALK ABOUT WORK**! You think that's easy, try it sometime! Why is this important? Do you realize that the people who are in charge of making your company successful become part of the process of your culture? They get "right-sized" and reengineered. But how many of them know each other past what they do for a living?

Who we are is not what we do, although the programming of today would not have us believe it is. It has long been a rule not to let friends work together because they will mess around. Nothing could be further from the truth. Yes, they will get on a tangent every now and then about their personal lives, but when one has to stay late or work extra to complete a project, guess who is first to step up and help – your friend! The one who cares about you.

Do your people care about each other? Will they step up to the plate with one another? Chances are they will not because your culture is not built on service or experience. Who will service or take care of them better? A stranger or a friend? The answer is obvious. But unless you provide time for the people side of your culture to develop, this benefit will never be yours.

Once the lunches take off, you can spread them to "after work" activities. You can even spread the practice to other levels of your organization. But be smart. One company we set down this path took their people bowling for lunch one day. Is this saying we value you by taking you bowling in a suit?

Process

We use the term "process" when describing the other half of corporate culture because it connotes an evolution. It suggests that your culture change is more than just a weekend retreat when everyone gets together and writes new vision statements. Every day, each of your employees must wake up thinking "How do I make my company's product stronger?" This culture change you are embarking on will take months, even years, depending on several factors.

The process side of your culture is the policies, the procedures, and the unwritten and unvisible rules within your company. The process discussion is where most of our clients get excited because they can understand what we are saying. How many books are there on the shelves of your local Barnes and Noble Bookstore or online at Amazon.com that are about the process or operational side of culture?

We expend thousands of hours and thousands of dollars making changes in our processes to increase profitability and customer service. And, truth be told, we usually see results. But the results are marginal at best, and this marginal success frustrates us, so we give up on the culture change.

What results can you expect from a culture change if you are only dealing with half of your corporate culture?

My experience has shown that this is where the riff occurs between the consultant and the company during a culture change process. The consultants tend to weigh themselves heavily to the people side of culture, whereas the company tends to lean towards the process side. This is easy to understand. There are two reasons this happens.

1. It is much easier for a company to deal with the process side. This is tangible, the factual. It can be measured and quantified.

2. The process side can have a measure of money attached to it. Although we made a small attempt at the beginning of this chapter to put a price tag on your culture, what part of that is people and what part is processed, will be debated for years. I can only tell you this. The companies like Southwest Airlines, Starbucks, Google, and Zappos all place equal importance on both sides. They make their decisions with their hearts and their heads, not just their wallets.

Obviously, we will shy away from the unknown. The people side of a culture is the unknown. We can cite hundreds and hundreds of examples of its value, but that would only make this book longer, and besides, this is something we all know is true. Why belabor the point? Besides, there is another burning question in your mind that needs attention.

How long will this culture change process take me?

And the answer is "What is the most popular question asked in regards to corporate culture change?" We have fond that three factors determine the timeframe. Each of these factors (outlined below) contribute in determining how long it takes to implement a culture change.

Declaring the culture change "implemented" is when the process side has done its part, and the people side has done its part, and the new identity of your company as an experience culture is established. Three critical factors determine your timing:

1. **The length of time your current management has been in place.** Who you are today is based on your management since management's job is to further the culture. Whatever the culture has been over the past few years is supported and reinforced by management. The longer they have been in place, the harder it will be to get them to change. It's not because they are "old dogs"; it's because when you change a culture, you are challenging not only the identity of the company but the identity of the employees as well. Management will not jump on board so easily if they find out it means they have to step out of their comfort zone and do things differently. Perhaps what you are trying to build is not for them. Which would you do in this case? Admit this and quit or would you stay and push against it?

2. **The number of employees in the company.** The larger the workforce, the longer it will take to change. Notice we did not say the harder, it will be to change. This is not the case at all. You can even expand this variable to a higher degree if your workforce is spread out over the whole country. When you have multiple locations, you will develop pockets of success. Some of them will sign up; others will not. You will find yourself jumping from location to location trying to keep what you gained in one location and trying to kick start another. You quickly become the plate spinner guy from the circus trying to keep all the plates spinning on the thin stick and letting none of them crash to the floor.

3.   **The length of time your current culture has been in place**. The elements that make up a corporate culture are deeply rooted in the people of the culture. Thinking back to our point that your corporate culture is a real, tangible (living, breathing) entity, you will understand that the older something is, the harder it is to get it to change. Just like Factor 1 above, the culture's age will determine how quickly it will adapt. A culture has a cycle of development that it follows. The more cycles that have been completed by your culture, the more time it will take to reprogram it (see "The Culture Cycle").

S. Truett Cathy, the founder of Chick Fi La, wanted the service (experience) in his fast food restaurants to be like that of a four-star hotel he stayed at frequently. He wanted the guests in his restaurants to feel like he did when he stayed at the hotel – the same **experience**. One of the things he noticed at this hotel was that whenever you said thank you, the staff always responded with "my pleasure." He wanted his stores to give the same response as part of the Chick Fi La experience. He wanted his customers to be waited on by employees who deemed it a pleasure to serve.

So, he held a meeting with his top executives and gave them the directive. They, in turn, took it to their direct reports which took it to their direct reports and so on and so on. After a month, Cathy visited some stores to see how will they were doing with delivering the "my pleasure" response. To his dismay, everyone was still saying "you're welcome." He went back to the office and gathered everyone again and gave the direction (firmer) this time.

The result? It took almost two years before everyone in the company was saying "my pleasure" versus you're welcome! But how can this be? Truett Cathy was the founder and the owner of the company. If he said make it so, it should be so, right? Logically, yes. But culturally, no. Remember it takes time to change your culture. The key to Chick Fi La's success was never giving up. Some companies might have turned back and said: "Forget it; it's not worth it." Later,

I'll share a story of a company who didn't stay the course and the negative impact that had on their culture change.

The Culture Assessment

To move forward with a new culture, you must first understand where your culture is now. This will do two things for you. First, it will help you plan your strategy. Knowing where your strengths and weaknesses are, will lead you to your implementation phase of culture change by defining what areas need the most immediate attention, and so on.

Second, it will help you know how difficult the task is going to be. If the experience culture you are trying to build has a totally different set of beliefs and values, then your time required will be much greater. This is a good thing. Do not let this part of the exercise disturb you. If you want to start over completely, that's okay.

The purpose of this next section is to help you determine the values, beliefs, behaviors, etc. of your current culture. There is a disclaimer here. I would highly recommend that you get some help with this part. (Of course, I would say that it's how I make our living. But this is not just a gratuitous plug for our company; it's a fact.) There are two reasons we would recommend outside help

1. **You are on the inside. An outsider can more clearly see the visible and, more importantly, the unvisible.**

2. **Any suggestions will be met with less resistance since they are from a neutral party.**

Both of these make total sense, and we are sure you can appreciate them. But this chapter is to help you get your license to drive, so we will briefly explain the steps I go through when assessing a culture. As in other sections, the intent here is not to make you experts on assessment, but to give you some insight as to what needs to happen.

And the truth is, what you are about to read – in fact, what you are reading in this entire book – is my exact process I follow when assisting a company in its culture change. So, while outside help does have its benefits as mentioned – YOU CAN DO IT! If you just follow these principles. Now, back to the culture assessment.

The purpose of the culture assessment is to look for these four things:

1. **The visible elements of your culture.**
2. **The unvisible elements of your culture.**
3. **The people side of your culture.**
4. **The process side of your culture.**

You are going to step back and take a good, long hard look at what these four areas are saying to your customers and your employees. There are two parts to the culture assessment process—the Interviews and the Tours. We weigh neither one more heavily than the other in their significance as a part of our assessment.

Interviews

We set up group interviews, at first making sure the groups meet the following criteria.

- **Some groups are level specific.** This refers to all hourly or front-line people in a group together and then all managers in a group together, etc. In these interviews, we are going to ask more level-specific questions. We will ask the same questions to each level and additional questions relating to the other levels to see how their perceptions and answers vary. It is amazing the impressions management has of hourly and vice versa.

- **Some groups are non-level-specific.** These groups will have representation from all levels within the company in the room together. We then compare the group dynamics and responses to the questions from the two types of groups. This gives us a control element to make sure we are getting an accurate read. Typically, in this combined group type, it is considerably less vocal and controversial. The front-line people will hold back, and management will control the discussion. This shows us there is a hierarchical culture right away. The front-line people are intimidated by management and do not speak freely in front of their bosses. This is not a sign of a Culturrific! company.

- **We keep all of the groups to less than 18 total people.** The larger the group, the more "filtered" the responses become. People feel more comfortable to share freely and openly in smaller, more intimate settings.

- **Try to hold the interviews off-site.** No matter how you prepare the group, they will still think there is a hidden camera somewhere, and they are being recorded or that their boss is hiding around the corner. This is the "anything-you-say-can-and-will-be-held-against-you-in-a-court-of-bosses" principle. In fact, I recommend against recording the group sessions for this very reason. Too many crime TV drama fans out there paranoid about the two-way mirror.

- **Keep all interviews confidential.** Never reveal who said what to anyone. It is okay to describe the comment as coming from an hourly or salaried person or even tying the comment to a specific job in your company. Keep all comments anonymous and make sure that the interviewees know this.

- **Never conduct written interviews.** Having people complete a questionnaire is very ineffective. When you cannot see their faces, you are not sure why they are making the comment. You may take it as humor, but they were serious. Also, when you watch the person respond, you get a feel for their conviction about what they are saying.

- **Involve as many people as possible**. In a company of 100-200 employees, we will also conduct enough group interviews to accommodate everyone who wants to participate. Your attendance will go up as the interviews continue. Word of mouth will do the advertising for you. If your company has several locations, you will need to conduct interviews at each location. Never let one location dictate for the rest!
- **Conduct one-on-one interviews with several people from each level.** Ask the same questions as you do in the group. This will give you another check for accuracy. If the responses are consistent, you are on the right track.

You can see where an outside person would be very beneficial here. The honest responses will increase dramatically if they are talking to someone who is not from the company. The more honest feedback you get, the greater your chances of your culture change succeeding. A note of advice here. Many companies will make the logical choice to have the HR department conduct these interviews. You know, the same guys who conduct all investigations that eventually lead to termination. Select people from "neutral" departments that will pose no threat to the employee to ensure you are getting unfiltered information.

The following is a list of the typical questions we will ask in the interviews to help you. We do not use them all every time.

- What was your first day like here?
- How much training do you go to each month?
- Is training important around here?
- What happens if you are late to work?
- Is it okay to make mistakes?
- Would you say you are empowered to make company decisions?
- Is there a division between management and hourly employees?
- Are there a lot of stressed out people in your company?

- Do you feel comfortable going to your boss with a problem?
- How often do you get together as a group?
- When did your company start?
- Who was the founder of your company?
- What is the purpose of your company?
- What gets the most time during a meeting?
- How often do you give out awards?
- Are innovation and new ideas thought highly of?
- Is more time spent on internal competition than external?
- Do you feel appreciated?
- What are some of the things your company values?
- How often do you get together outside of work?
- What do you have to do to get promoted?
- Why would someone choose your company versus all the others?
- What is your service really like?
- Are customer comments (positive or negative) shared with you?
- What is the employee experience like working here?
- How would you describe the customer experience here?

You can see where we are going with these questions. I never directly mention the word culture or explain to them what I am looking for. This will only confuse the issue. I interpret from the responses to these questions what the culture is. Some of the questions above may seem like we are leading the witness and you could predict the answer. This is true. But remember, you are asking the executives these questions as well. Some of the so-called obvious questions become hard quickly.

Be careful not to embarrass anyone or put anyone on the spot. A VP who does not know when the company started will be very mortified sitting with the hourly employees. He will feel stupid, and when this happens, this person usually decides to resist whatever you try later in your culture change. Try to avoid this.

Move your questions around the room – never in the predictable rotation style, rather in a jumping style from side to side. Make sure that you keep copious notes of the responses and that your scribe for the interviews keeps accurate records of what positions attended. Knowing who was represented helps you to understand the responses. You will need to filter some of the hourly responses given to you. Obviously, for many who are just working with their hands and their feet, there is nothing the company could do that would be right. Make it fun and entertaining. Be honest with what you are doing – simply gaining an understanding of the company.

Tours

In between the interviews, we will walk the physical structure of the company to look for the **visible signs** of the culture. It never fails. Every company that says people are their most important asset, have few signs in the building to prove this is true. Once again, their identity does not fit their image. The first place I look is the break room or lunchroom. How is it decorated? What is the food like? Would you be proud to have your customers visit and eat here? Usually, when I ask this question, the manager giving the tour laughs at the joke he thinks we just made. Poor manager.

On tour with a large oil and gas firm in Dallas, we were shown the employee lunchroom. Wolfgang Puck operated it. Now that's amazing. (And probably out of 98% of companies budgets.) But it does display the value of the employee.

We'll look at what the signs and memos next to the employee time clock say. Are there lots of "effective immediately" memorandums? What is this saying to your employee? I'll tell you.

The memo might as well look like the one below because this is certainly how it will be read. People will make mistakes, and people will do things incorrectly, and you will have to publish memos and other bulletins to keep everyone informed. But, you can do it with experience in mind.

To: all Employees

From: Management
Date: Everyday

Effective immediatly, You guys suck!

Thank You.

The memo is the last form of communication. The first is verbal. If you are holding bi-monthly meetings with all your employees, this is the time to explain new policies and why they are necessary. Touch the hearts and the heads at every possible opportunity!

I then walk the offices and look for more visible signs. Is the work area clean? Dirty? Organized? Are there pieces of scotch tape or old staples on the wall from the last three people who held the job? How are they decorated? Are the walls filled with personal pictures or team pictures? Are there signs that this place is like a family? In the Port Orleans resort at Disney World, all of the pictures in the guestrooms are of actual families of the housekeeping cast. In another company we worked with, we changed the traditional meeting room names and instead named the rooms in the hotel for "retired service heroes" of the property. While most hotels name the rooms after local landmarks, this one named them after their service elite. How about that for hearts and heads?

How about outside activities? Are there any? How often? What kinds? We look in the public spaces as well as the private. We examine the policy manuals. When were they written? Did humans or androids (or worse yet, lawyers) write them? (No explanation needed, I'm sure.) We especially look at the training materials and the training itself. This is one of the key questions that I ask in the interviews and then follow up with during our tours.

"What types of training did you receive when you first started?" If you are like most companies we have worked with, you have the "behind" training system. As soon as you see their behind hit the doorway out of your office, training is over. Good luck. Find your way through it and do your best. We are all counting on you. We find this to be a consistent theme that must change for your culture to be experience driven.

Some consulting firms suggest personality-typing analysis be done as a part of the assessment as well. This will help you understand who you will be working with. However, these assumptions are very dangerous in the hands of amateurs. They can quickly assign labels to people, which you will not be able to recover from. We have used different forms of these in the past, but keep a close reign on the results. We know how to interpret them and what their purpose is for. Be careful.

What's it worth to you?

After your culture assessment is complete, you are then ready to decide what steps need to be taken to make your new culture a reality. Now comes the tough part. What resources (people, company time, money, etc.) are you going to dedicate to this culture change effort? One of the more common reactions we get is "We cannot afford to put him or her on the culture change effort. They are too important to us where they are!" Is that a message or what? This is your current culture talking, not the new one. But as long as you listen to it, you are stalling the bus.

Another measurement is the amount of money budgeted to this effort. **Most companies set aside about 5-10% of their re-engineering budget to training. Unfortunately, training is the most important element of this process**. And the type of training is not the simple, inexpensive type. You have to make a statement, and you need to use newer more experiential forms of training, and these forms cost money. You can recognize the value by analyzing where management has put the money – behind the process side of the culture (through re-engineering procedures) or the people side of the culture (training and education). Where is your money?

The overall goal of the assessment is to determine the current state of your company and its culture. Then as you begin your planning, you can begin with the desired end state in mind and work your way back to the current or existing state.

There are three other critical points you need to know before you can start your planning. These points make up the next three sections in this book. They are:

1. The Culture Cycle - The most important part of these lessons.
2. Self-Esteem - Understanding the role self-esteem plays in your culture change;
3. Everything Speaks - an explanation of this term I keep referring too.

These three principles will help you in shaping your new culture. You must have a decent feel for what an experience culture is and how it develops to be able to change yours and make it Culturrific!. Let's drive on.

The Culture Cycle

To change a culture, you must start at the beginning – the programming. You can modify any culture for awhile, but to initiate true change, you must start with the way it is programmed.

In the last section, we stated that one of the five key elements of an experience culture was behavior. You must instill new behaviors in your company to make it work. What your new behaviors need to be will be based on what the current ones are. To understand the current ones, you need to know how you got here. We also made the statement that each of the five culture elements (behavior, folklore, communication, values, and beliefs) are **interdependent**.

A culture develops over time. It is not an overnight process. It must be influenced time and time again before it takes shape. When a company is founded, its corporate culture is like an infant at birth. It is a living, breathing part of the company, which takes years to develop fully. Just as there is a cycle of development for an infant, there is also a definitive cycle that a culture follows as part of its development. When you understand this cycle, you will understand how your culture grew to become what it is today and, more importantly, you will know how to change it.

Exhibit 32 shows a snapshot of what this cycle looks like. Before we begin our journey through the cycle, there are two principles of this cycle theory that you must accept before it will work for you.

1.   **This is a cycle. It repeats itself daily.** These are not stages over time: rather, they are a daily routine that feeds your culture - either reinforcing it or modifying it. When your company first started, this cycle was more of a stage development process. Today you have a mature culture, which has already developed. You are looking to change this "adult, " and the change follows the same cycle.

2.   **If this is a cycle, then it must follow the sequence outlined.** You cannot let the people on the bus until the door is open and you cannot start the bus until there is gas in the engine. These facts about your culture bus are true for your culture cycle as well. There are no shortcuts in this process, so do not try.

Exhibit 32

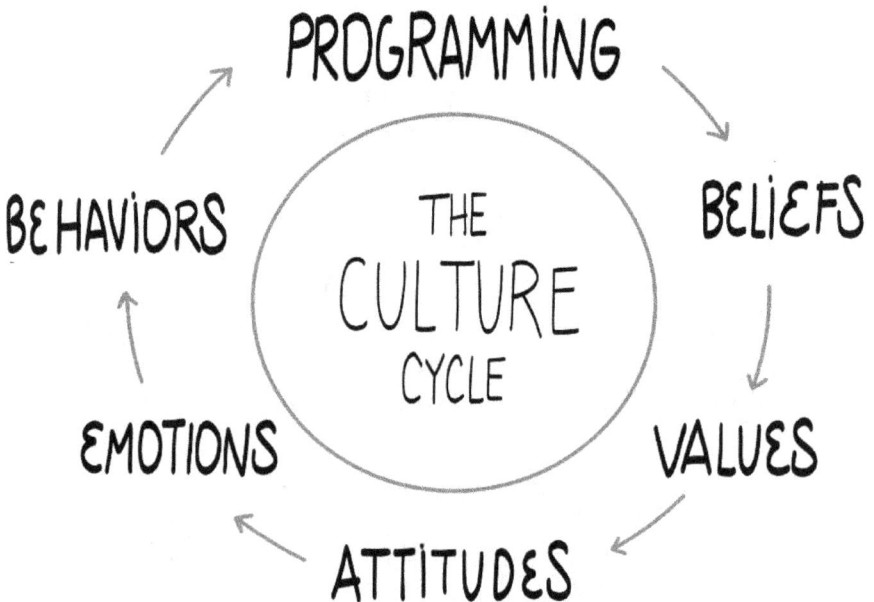

PROGRAMMING

BEHAVIORS

THE
CULTURE
CYCLE

BELIEFS

EMOTIONS

VALUES

ATTITUDES

The culture cycle states that your culture's programming determines your beliefs, and beliefs determine your values, and your values determine your attitudes, and your attitudes determine your emotions, and your emotions determine your culture's behaviors. As you can see, the cycle builds upon itself with each step. You cannot have a set of values until you have determined your belief system. You cannot control attitudes until you understand the values of your culture. We will deal with each part of the cycle individually.

Programming

Sometimes, more commonly known as conditioning, the input your employees get on a daily basis starts the cycle. Here is where the rubber meets the road. At first, this is a great asset to you; but, when you have a mature culture, the parts of the cycle that follow will filter all of the programming.

What are some forms of programming? Well, first of all, Everything Speaks. Everything you do, every sign you make, every rule you pass, every policy you establish, every speech you give (you get the point) is part of the programming of your culture. We will talk more about the Everything Speaks concept in a chapter to come. For now, we will keep our programming definition simple.

Going back to the infant analogy again, we can see that what the infant becomes is what guidance or programming it is given. We all know the stories of the teachers who were given three different classes to work with. The first teacher was told that her students were slow and no matter how hard she tried, they would never learn at a regular pace. The second teacher was told that her students were average. She should challenge them a little bit, but not too hard since they would never be the smartest – after all, they were average. The third teacher was told that her students were geniuses. She better challenge them like they had never been challenged before. And if they complained, don't let up on them. That's just what geniuses do.

After the semester, the students were tested and sure enough, the first class of kids – the slow ones – never made it as far as the other two. The second class of average students did, well – average. But the third class of students – the geniuses – did awesomely. They blew everyone away. By now you have probably figured out that this was a setup. All of the students in each class were the same – average. But based on the programming the teachers had received, their expectations of the students were different. Their programming determined their beliefs about the kids, and eventually, their behavior showed it.

When the "slow" kids said they didn't get it, the teacher behaved as if it wasn't their fault and in so doing programmed the students that they were slow. But when the geniuses complained, their teacher wouldn't back down, and her behavior programmed them that they were smart.

Your managers are teachers of your employees. You don't have to be in a classroom to learn. What are your manager's expectations of their employees? If they are part-time college kids, what does the culture tell the manager to think? Interesting, isn't it?

This programming has taken on a whole new state in recent years with the rise of social media and "fake news." Anyone can express an opinion – right or wrong – and it is taken as informed, researched, and true. The fact is, anyone can write a blog. And anyone can screw with Wikipedia. The job of culture change only got more difficult when people took to the internet to share their thoughts.

Beliefs

How you believe today is based on what you have been told through programming in the past. If you have been taught that stealing is stealing and any form of it is bad and should be punished, then that is what you will believe. This whole culture cycle concept is easy to grasp because it relates so well to you as an individual in your life.

Perhaps you grew up in a different "culture" that felt stealing was really only stealing if it was something you could go to jail for. Anything else is no big deal. Just compare the rules differences between the major sports to see the different value systems. Drugs and "doping" have been a major topic in the NBA, MLB, and NFL, but in some of these leagues, a little is okay and it others nothing is permitted. However, in all of them, what matters is if you get caught. While the policy may be severe in punishment, most players know that it will get reduced or even dropped by the union rep. So why worry?

Many corporate cultures have speeches about the importance of training or customer service, but do they really believe it? **More importantly, does the culture really believe it?** It's time for a sincerity check.

Your beliefs are the strong personal convictions of your culture. They are more than just ideas. They are grounded principles. Based on your past experiences within your company, when you introduce this culture change, the belief might be "Just wait awhile, and it will all go away. He just read another Forbes article or attended another one of those seminars, that's all."

Keep in mind that with beliefs, you have to investigate what is really going on and not what is in writing. I spoke at the "100 Best Companies to Work For" conference a few years ago. I got to have lunch with Martin Brossman, the creator of the instrument and study that is used to determine the Top 100. He told me that the reason most companies will never make it to the Top 100 is the beliefs of their culture. His example was paternity leave. Many companies outside the Top 100 would look at what the Top 100 were doing and then try and imitate with certain practices or benefits for employees. Paternity leave was one of the main ones that got emulated.

But it never took off. **You see the men in the company didn't "believe" (trust) that their jobs would be there when they got back even though the policy said they would.** Plus, there was such a paranoia about being gone for too long that no one ever took advantage of the benefit. The culture's beliefs didn't support it, and therefore the employees saw it as no value.

Values

Your beliefs determine your values. What you believe about something determines how much value you will place on it. Here is where we start to develop customer or employee experience value in your culture.

As we work our way through the cycle, we will see if you truly value customers and employees – if the experience is a real concern for you. If a belief is a strong personal conviction, then a value is the worth we place on that belief. The stronger our conviction to the belief, the greater the value we will place on it. Therefore, the stronger a value it will be to your culture.

For now, let's go back to our stealing analogy. If you were programmed that stealing is stealing, then all of your possessions are valuable to you. You place great value (worth) on what you have – even if it's just a candy bar. You will have the same value on the candy bar that you have in your house. It is yours and should be respected.

We often hear the term "The customer is always right!" If this is a true belief of your culture, then care and service of the customer will be a value in your culture. But if you are like most companies, the customer is king mentality is a slogan, not a belief. This plays out when one of your employees blows off a customer because they are annoying them. No value here.

Attitudes

Your culture's value system will determine the attitudes that will develop as a result of an action in your company. For example, if you believe time is a very precious commodity and it is a value in your culture, then your employee's attitudes towards someone who is late to a meeting will be negative.

This late-to-a-meeting analogy is a great one because time management is certainly preached in most cultures, but it is neither believed nor valued. I know this from the amount of time I have spent waiting in lobbies for the people we are consulting with!

But what about your candy bar? If you were the "by the book thinker," and someone walked by your desk and took your candy bar what would your attitude be? If you were the "stealing is only wrong if it's something big like a car" thinker, what would your attitude be? They would be very different, wouldn't they? The "by the book" person would certainly react based on their value and belief structure – negatively. They would "cop" an attitude and then get a cop.

Three basic attitudes appear here. They are positive, negative and ambivalent. As they sound, the positive attitude will translate into a positive emotion in the next phase of the cycle. A negative attitude then will elicit a negative emotion. And finally, the ambivalent attitude is Switzerland – you know the country that is always neutral on all issues!

An ambivalent attitude is neither positive nor negative and is very unpredictable in the cycle and truth, **can be more destructive because you do not know how to program this person effectively**. Plus, their emotions that come as a result are very unpredictable as well.

Emotions

The attitude that your mind develops then begins to translate into an emotional response or feeling. If you have been waiting for someone to start the meeting for 15 minutes, your attitude said, "this is wrong." Now, your emotions are starting to "flair up, " and you're getting more perturbed by the minute.

Emotions are tough because they cloud our judgment and exaggerate the situation – so much so sometimes that our behavior is irrational. The candy bar thief? Well, let's just hope that the person he or she has so ruthlessly violated never finds them! Meanwhile, the other people (the car thinkers) cannot understand why someone would get so emotional over a stupid candy bar. This person should obviously seek professional help.

We are a very emotional society. We are not afraid to tell people how we feel about them and the bus they rode in on. *You must cast people in service roles who have strong control over their emotions*. But no matter how controlled they are, if the belief and value system of your culture sends "attitude" through, guess what!

Behavior

Finally, all of the cycles is complete, and you take action. The late guy is strapped to the flipchart, his shirt and tie removed and each of you takes turns writing, "I will never be late again" in permanent marker on his chest. That's right, the behavior part of our cycle is when the cycle is complete, and **we act**.

With so many parts preceding it, you can easily see why the behavior in your culture is so revealing. How we behave or the actions we take outwardly are a direct result of the culture cycle inwardly.

So what your organization's culture is today, in essence how the people perform for you, is based on a cycle started years ago when you were born (started) and restarts every morning they report to work. Some authors would speak of sub-cultures, the smaller cultures of individual departments and their dynamics on the whole. While there is merit to these thoughts, this level of diagnosis is a little much for us. It's hard enough to keep up with the big picture, let alone a whole bunch of little ones.

But the merit to their argument is proven in this cycle. Take our Loss Prevention people for example. Obviously, the programming they have received over time has taught them to believe that stealing is WRONG regardless of the dollar amount of the item. Therefore, they really value their candy bar. Their attitude is one of "you better not touch my candy bar" because if you do, they will get very emotional and probably see that you get five to ten upstate.

This sub-culture mentality is at work here. We could go on and give more examples from all over the company. The accounting group sees themselves as protectors of the company coffers, whereas the sales group sees the accounting group as "anal retentive overly stressed about the little stuff" people. For purposes of your journey, though, these dynamics are not of great significance.

Culture change is a balance of art and science. The cycle above makes clear sense. This book is not about saving the world, just your culture.

Probably the best example of a company's culture cycle at play is in the sales game. You hire a new hot shot that comes charging out of the gate and posts awesome numbers for the first few months. But then suddenly, their performance starts to lower and so do their numbers. Pretty soon they are producing at about the same level as everyone else on the team. Haven't we all tried to figure this one out before? You know the answer. The culture cycle kicked in.

Immediately, when the new salesperson hits the floor, he was charged. His programming to this point had been "You the man!" and his behavior lived up to that expectation. But the programming of the culture started to kick in and eventually, day after day after day of everyone and everything around the new guy saying, "You can't sell here. This economy is dead. Our product is not as good as our competitions." This programming becomes this man's belief. He starts to believe everything being said to him by the others. And their actions (more programming) supported everything they were saying because they were not selling like he was. Oh, sure they used to sell like him and they would if they got transferred to the other store, but...

In just a few months, this fireball of a salesman was drug to the ground in a fizzle. His attitude changed "No one is going to buy from me." His emotions changed, "I don't want to talk to them, they will just reject me." And his behavior changed, "Hey, has anyone seen the new guy? This is the third time he's been late this week!"

When we say that your culture is a living, breathing animal, we aren't kidding!

The Great Culture Change Mistake

The most common mistake we see companies making today is that they are trying to change their culture without following the cycle. For example, there is Walmart. Out of nowhere, this retailer came up to be the dominant player eclipsing the one-time leader (and now bankrupt and all but gone) K-Mart.

When Walmart's success started to be noticed by the country, the leaders of other companies did what all great leaders do. They sent one of their people to go and find out how Walmart was doing it! Find the magic potion, bring it to me, and I will rule the World!

We are always looking for the next quick fix. This is why the majority of culture changes or reengineering efforts fail. We ignore the whole cycle and its impact. One of the things that Sam Walton used to do when he visited the stores was to get the employees to cheer. They would lead pep rallies just like in high school before the big homecoming game. For Walmart, every day is a homecoming. One of the ways their culture celebrates and communicates this is through cheering. You could always tell where Sam Walton was in the store on his tour because the cheers would rise from the employees.

The spies saw this and took it back to their leader. "We have found the secret," they said. "We must get our people to cheer!" So all across the country, people started cheering. Pep rallies started rising. And the companies were seeing some positive effect from these new initiatives.

It didn't take long, though, for these initiatives to lose their charm and impact. "Perhaps we need a new cheer?" thought the leaders. So they toured the country again, hitting every location and every department all in the name of rallying the employees to the great company cause. And again, they had a slight effect on performance. But it still didn't last. Why? Because they were ignoring the cycle!

These companies had fallen into the most common trap. They were trying to influence the **attitudes of the company**. They came into the middle of the cycle at the attitude part and tried to change the culture. The problem is that when the cycle starts to repeat itself, the beliefs and values of the culture kick back in and they change the attitudes back.

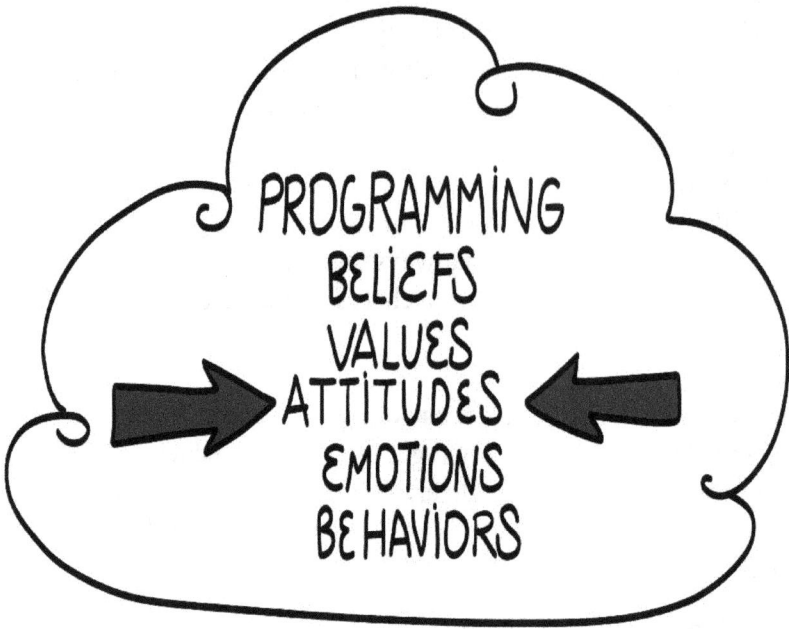

PROGRAMMING
BELIEFS
VALUES
→ ATTITUDES ←
EMOTIONS
BEHAVIORS

My favorite employee directive is "Mister; you better change your attitude if you want to stay around here!" This blessed method of motivational management has such a force of influence on the employee that they immediately respond, start to carry a positive attitude to work, and are happy and smiling all the time for about three days. Then, they are back to their old ways of doing things. Why? Again the culture cycle.

You see, the cheering was a way to impact the attitudes of the Walmart culture, but it was just one part of a very large process. It was also a part that was culturally acceptable. Would your company employees jump up on their chairs with enthusiasm and cheer at the top of their lungs if you asked them to? Or would they look at you like you had lost your mind? Walmart's culture supported this type of behavior. It was part of their beliefs and their values that they should cheer. Walmart was not yelling to pump air into the lungs of its employees; they were yelling to **pump soul into their culture**.

This is probably the most important lesson in the book. (You know if that's the case, I probably should save it for last, so you will read the whole book.) **If you want to change your culture, you must start at the beginning of your cycle.** This will become important for you as you start to define your new experience culture.

How many stories have we read about the online companies like Google and Zappos with their massage chairs and go-kart races at lunch? These are amazing employee experiences and part of their culture, but can you imagine sitting in a budget meeting with your CFO and explaining the expense for massages and go karts? These cultures were built from the ground up and designed with these ideas in place. **Be careful not to copy someone's culture that is not relevant to yours.**

Recently, there was another great example of culture change disaster. Ron Johnson orchestrated a retail phenomena in Apple stores. Apple stores have the highest dollar per square foot of any retailer ever. JC Penny lured Ron away from Apple and asked him to remake JC Penney into a brand like Apple.

When Ron arrived, he found a culture of complacency. He found a retailer lacking vision. But he had a plan. He wanted to end all of the ups and downs of retail sales driven by sales events and instead of smooth out the selling curve by offering low prices every day. He called this Square Deal pricing (taken from Penny's square logo.) In other words, like Ron Hill and I so many years before, he wanted to reshape the culture of retail.

He hired a high-powered ad agency, and they went to work convincing the buying public that they did not need to wait for a sale, that they could get a square deal every day at Penneys.

But it failed – horribly! Some will tell you it's the customer. Others will tell you it's the economy. But I will tell you it was the culture. Remember that culture of complacency I mentioned. Ron was effective in changing merchandising and marketing strategies. In fact, I think his vision was revolutionary and would have worked. **But he forgot the most important element – the culture.**

No effort was made to change the culture. And therefore when a customer would come into JC Penney and ask about square deal pricing, the employees were not on board. In fact, they worked against it.

When a customer would ask, "so you really don't have sales anymore?" The employee would say, "well actually we do have sales we just don't publish them in the ads anymore. Every third Friday we mark all of the items down that have not been selling So if you come back then, you can get a sale."

Now, honestly, I imagine many of these employees were not sharing this information to sabotage the new CEO's plans. In fact, they were probably just being friendly. The problem is that little time was spent on changing the culture. The ad campaign started quickly way before the employees were ready for it.

Just like the story of Walmart above where the company tried to change the culture by entering into the middle of the cycle, Ron Johnson and his team tried to change the culture from the outside of the company. They ignored the Culture Cycle, and the result was Ron being fired and a complete reversal of his strategy. Sad. I liked Square Deal pricing and the new merchandise it was bringing into the stores.

In the last chapter, we gave you the elements of a corporate culture. In future ones, we will have you define each of those elements for your new experience culture. This means you will have to decide what "values" will be important to your new culture. In other words, to build a Culturrific! team delivering a remarkable experience to every customer every time, what values must your culture espouse to get you there?

Using the culture cycle, you cannot simply assign values and pass them out on a memo or email. You must follow the cycle. You have to first replace the old values of your culture, and to do that you must formulate new beliefs in your culture, and to do that you must change their programming. Obviously, the beliefs are the toughest part because it takes a while to convince someone you are serious.

The late guy to the meeting will still probably be late again if he "believes" they were just fooling. The company can pass a new policy under the guise of culture change that anyone late to a meeting will have to sing a karaoke song in front of the group. But if, in the past, being late was commonplace, then that is what the value of the culture is and a new policy will have little impact…until they have sung a few times and find out you are serious. You see, every karaoke song is a form of programming the culture. Which means it does work. Starting to get the hang of it?

By now you should be seeing why this is so difficult a task to undertake and why the first line in Chapter One said, "Culture change is not for the weak of heart!" Defining values and deciding your new purpose and mission – piece of cake. Getting them to translate to behavior – BIG CAKE! (A cake the size of the Empire State Building.) But hey, that's why you're here. To become a champion cake baker and bus driver and soon you will be. Read on.

Culture and Self-Esteem

People draw the majority of their self-esteem from their job.

It's a fact, no matter how hard we try to deny it, that as humans we create and base our self-esteem on outside influences. Every great motivational speaker from Napoleon Hill to Denis Waitley to Tony Robbins taught us that we must take control of our self-esteem and what programs it if we are to be successful.

To have this discussion, we need a working definition of self-esteem. Our friends at the American Heritage Dictionary define it as 'confidence.' With this definition, I'm not too impressed with our friends. We find it easier to understand if you deal with each side of the hyphen.

The word esteem, when used as a verb (as it is here), means 'to hold in high regard.' When we give something esteem, we hold it in high regard and give it great importance. When you put the two together, your definition becomes "to hold one's self in high regard."

This is certainly easier said than done. Most troubled people are such because on the outside they profess to hold themselves in high regard, but on the inside, they know the truth. You probably know a lot of these people. These are people who try to put on an outward display of their positive self-esteem. This effort actually induces more stress on them than if they would just face the truth.

In the last chapter, we discussed the culture cycle (programming, beliefs, values, attitudes, emotions, and behaviors). You could use this model for the development of a person's self-esteem as well. All the psychologists tell us that our fears and behaviors are learned over time. As a matter of fact, as a baby, we are born with just two fears – the fear of heights and the fear of sudden loud noises. How many of us still have just those two fears today?

As people, we want to belong to something – a group, a team, a club, a gang, a church. We spend our whole lives trying to fit in. The programming we receive in life is what shapes who we are. Part of that programming is the impact of your company's culture. **There is a definite connection between what we do for a living and our self-esteem.**

The problem is that we learn this connection between our self-esteem and our job very young in life and it becomes more than a connection to us – it becomes a definition of who we are. This is a very powerful statement, one that needs proof.

I wanted to test this presupposition, so we visited a 2nd grade class of children one day to talk about "Career Day." If you do not have kids of your own or your children have warped your mind so that you cannot remember back that far, these 2nd graders are about eight years old.

Before we had any discussions, we told them we wanted to play a game. We pre-made five signs and tied strings to the top corners so the signs could be draped around the children's necks. On each of the signs was a job type. We hung one card around each child's neck and asked them to line up in order of importance. Who did they think was the most important? This person should stand on the left and work their ranking to the right.

The signs read:

Doctor, Teacher, Lawyer, Garbage Man, and Farmer

Here is what happened. The two children labeled Doctor and Lawyer started to argue and push a little as to who was most important. They both felt they were the most important and should be first. But the teacher knew that he was not as important as the doctor or lawyer and immediately took his place third in line without saying a word. The farmer, knowing that people who wore ties or dressed up for work were more important, took her place fourth in line. The teacher and the farmer both stood quietly not saying a word. We looked for the garbage man, but he was not in line. Instead, the little boy with the label "Garbage Man" was sitting to the side quietly sobbing.

As a tear ran down his face, I questioned him what was wrong. "Please, please, I don't want to be the garbage man! I want to be important!"

If we were looking for proof that a person draws the majority of their self-esteem from his or her job, it was there in the teary eyes of that little boy. I have conducted this experiment other times mixing up the signs. I have tried nurse in place of a doctor, factory worker in place of a farmer and expanded into third graders. Each time the results were the same. There were always two kids fighting over; first, the middle children knew their place, and the last place person always cried foul.

Where do we learn this? Television? Movies? Video Games? Role models? Parents? The answer is D - all the above. The impact all of this media or personal contact has on a child's life only gets stronger as we grow older. And with the advent of tablets and other mobile devices and video games, it's just getting worse. But the purpose of this book is not to address this problem with our society. I'll save that for another book (and probably another author.)

The important part for you to remember is that people draw the majority of their self-esteem from their job. This means the more fulfilling your employees feel their role is in your company, the higher their self-esteem. And we all know the connection between a high self-esteem and work productivity and quality.

It's important to know about this connection for two reasons.

1. **It helps you to understand why the culture cycle is so important**. As addressed in the last chapter, when you try to influence your people and your culture by coming into the middle of the cycle, you only make matters worse. You may have a temporary effect, but the patterns are developed already.

2. **Studies show that people will protect their self-esteem at all costs**. This does not mean they will keep a healthy self-esteem. People will put all of their energies into trying not to lose ground or, in essence, maintaining their current self-esteem rather than trying to raise it.

As people, we eventually accept the role we have in life and spend our days rationalizing it and convincing ourselves that this is the way life's supposed to be. Psychologists call this our comfort zone. The hardest thing to do is push someone out of his or her comfort zone and get them to raise performance. But this is exactly what you are doing. I remember a CEO telling me one time in the middle of assisting him with his company's culture change "I'm so far out of my comfort zone, I can't even see it anymore." That told me we were on the right track.

Follow this pattern. If the culture cycle is the development of your culture, then it stands to reason that your current culture is somewhat of a comfort zone for your employees. They may moan, gripe and complain about their current work conditions, but these people could get 40 hours pay for 30 hours worked and still find something to complain about. Why? Because that is who they are. This is the regard they hold for themselves. That is what their current state of self-esteem is telling them. And let's be honest, often times people become "comfortable" when they are complaining.

So if a person draws the majority of his or her self-esteem from his or her job and their job is actually defined by your corporate culture, then their self-esteem is determined and impacted by your culture. As if you weren't carrying enough weight on your shoulders, we have now added the self-esteem of every employee to the load!

We make this connection to help you understand where the employees are coming from. They will resist you in your efforts. Guarantee it. This helps you figure out why. We will deal with this point more in the last chapter "Getting to the Heart of the Matter."

Please know, I am not telling you all of this to make you amateur psychologists. Do not go out and buy a couch to place in your office for your next set of employee reviews! Ultimately, a person is in control of his or her self-esteem. The culture and the company will definitely impact it, but to what level is still up to the individual.

I have heard many stories about people who work jobs that most of us would consider demeaning, but they have a smile on their face and take such pride in their work. Bill Pollard in <u>The Soul of the Firm</u> describes the majority of his company's people as being this way. ServiceMaster cleans toilets as a business. But the people who do it, work with pride because they are members of a culture which values them as people and strives to maintain an environment for their employee's development of a healthy self-esteem.

These are the types of people you want on your Culturrific! team. They have learned to disconnect who they are from what they do. Unfortunately, you cannot go out and fire everyone and start over. If you could, you would not be reading this book.

You must understand what you are dealing with when you start to mess with corporate culture. Those 2nd graders did not learn to devalue someone who picks up garbage from school. They learned it from their peers, media, and family. It took years of influence and culture to make the rules. The hierarchical structure "ring cultures" have taught us all that there are two types of jobs— menial jobs and important (glamorous) jobs.

By the way, a "ring culture" is one where the company promotes from within and the only way to get to the top is by kissing the ring of the top guys in respect for their making it. Sort of a Godfather thing. If you have this type of culture, I pray for you. Someone who spent 20 years kissing everyone's ring to get there will not easily give up the pleasure of now being the "ring kissee." They will be a big challenge for you. Why? You know the answer. They draw their self-esteem from the amount of kisses they receive.

Self-esteem is linked to service and experience

If people draw the majority of their self-esteem from their job, then you have a responsibility to build a culture that allows them to do so—a culture of nurturing, praising and accountability. If your people are going to serve the customer the way you want them to, they need to feel good about themselves when they do it. **It's the key to the customer experience.**

A few years ago, a company by the name of Performance Group Inc. in Dallas, Texas did a survey of 1,000 people who had just changed jobs. They asked these people to tell them why they left their last position. Guess what the number one answer was?

If you are being honest, you probably said money, as did I at first. But the overwhelming answer was "lack of recognition." What were these people saying? They were saying they worked in a culture that did not value them and did nothing for their self-esteem, so they left. (By the way, this survey was of Gen X and Baby Boomer workers. In the next chapter, I'll talk about how the answer is still the same with the next generations.)

Think about yourself. You might be working a position now that pays less than the last one you held. Why did you do this? The same reason these people in the survey did. You want to work for a place that allows you to come home to your family and be proud of what you do and who you do it for.

The person is always more important than the position.

Remember that!

This pattern started when you were a little kid. You wanted to be an astronaut or a fireman or a ballerina – you wanted to be someone important and what made them important was what they did for a living. Make what your company and its employees do for a living the most important job in the world. There are no small parts, just small actors.

The real resolution is for a person to learn NOT to draw their self-esteem from their job. But this book is not about what you can't control, but what you can! Culture change is an odds game. You must play the odds or percentages sometimes. I put this chapter in this book to help you understand the basis for many of the things that I suggest. **An experience culture must be a self-esteem-enhancing machine**. Every policy, every award, every speech, every process you put into place will impact the self-esteem of your employees.

As you try to capture the hearts and heads of your employees, you will find that the main reason you only get their hands and feet can be traced to the regard they hold of themselves. You have adults who have spent their lives being programmed to settle for less than what they are worth and for less than they can achieve. And more importantly for you, less than what they can deliver!

A group of scientists built a fish tank for an experiment that had a clear wall in the center dividing the tank into two sections. On one side they placed a plump, juicy mackerel. On the other side, they placed a barracuda. The Barracuda could see the mackerel, but it could not get to it. Within the first minute, the hungry barracuda spotted the mackerel and swam headfirst towards it and plowed into the center pane of glass. He swam away dizzied for a while, but when the barracuda regained its senses, he went for the mackerel again! And like before, he slammed into the center pane of glass. This had continued for quite some time before the barracuda decided "This hurts!" (It takes people a few knocks in the head sometimes to get it as well.)

___

The barracuda's behavior began to change. It would see the mackerel and swim headfirst towards it, but it would turn right before it hit the center glass. This became a pattern – the barracuda would see the mackerel, think "lunch!" and swim towards it, but right before it knocked its head, it would turn and swim away. This occurred enough times that eventually the scientists were able to take the center pane of glass out of the tank so that the Barracuda *could* get to the mackerel and guess what happened? The barracuda swam right up to the same point, turned and swam away! It kept swimming right up to that point, turning and swimming away never getting the mackerel.

As people, we have been conditioned or programmed to settle for less. I know that it is extraordinary to suggest a company be responsible for an employee's self-esteem, but there you go again buying that couch for your office. I am not supporting that you try to influence or control their self-esteem. I want to make you aware of the undercurrents at play in a culture change. When you encounter resistance or reluctance to your new ideas, understand where it is coming from. The source is much deeper than plain stubbornness.

If you want to capture their hearts and their heads, you must develop a culture that cares for them as people and provides a nurturing environment for their self-esteem. How do you do that, you ask? Keep reading.

Culture and The New Generations

"In my day, we used to work for money, and we liked it."

Probably not a more fitting quote to begin this chapter than that one. Since the first edition of this book, two major things have happened. One, the internet is starting to catch on. Two, a whole generation has shifted in the workforce.

Today, Millennials make up the largest percentage of the workforce. Baby Boomers are all but gone, and the Gen Xers are not far behind. And Gen Z, the generation after Millennials, are beginning to enter the workforce as well and when they do, they are expected to be about 1.5 Million larger in size than the Millennial group. In fact, by 2020, it is estimated that one-third of the US population will be Gen Z. So you can see that a major shift is coming — in fact is already here.

Gen Z is best defined as people born 1996 or later. Millennials are now getting older ranging from 22 — 40 years of age. Millennials grew up with technology as siblings, but Gen Z was born into a post-digital world that makes technology the center of their lives and not an accessory.

This is significant because now because it changes who we approach our businesses. The employees in these next generations want something different from their job and employer (and the culture) than the generations before them. These differences have a direct impact on corporate culture. Or better said, your corporate culture better be ready for these differences if you want to recruit and retain quality employees.

You might think that with all that youthful energy in the workforce that great things will happen. However, according to a study completed by Grovo, 60% of all millennial employees in retail LEAVE within the first 3 years. This turnover costs retailers thousands of dollars each time. With this group making up such a large percentage of the employees now, retailers have to adjust their approach. And if it hits retailers like this, it will your Company too.

The biggest problem is that the core values of these generations are very different than the core values of most companies today. True, we read about Zappos and other companies who are experiencing huge success with the Millennial workforce, but they are the exception, not the rule.

In comparing research from Grovo and Deloitte (as well as others), we can determine five core values the next generations look for in an employer. When they find them, they stay. When the company doesn't have them - they leave. These values are:

1. **Development**

2. **Meaning**

3. **Autonomy**

4. **Efficiency**

5. **Transparency**

Let's examine each one closely.

Development

This group is craving training and equipping. They want to grow and get better. They want to know they are improving their state in the company and the main way they gauge this is through training.

The biggest thing you can do for this group is to value education the way they do. They want to know more and more. They want to grow - not so they leave you, but so they achieve personal pride. So, resist the fear that you will spend a bunch of money on this group in development only to have them leave you for someone else. If you invest in them, they will return to it. The only reason they want to leave is if they stop growing.

According to the Deloitte study, 71% of Millennials who plan to leave their current job list being unhappy with their leadership development' as the reason. The younger generations desire to be in leadership (not much different than their predecessors), and the cultures that nurture that development will foster employee loyalty. In other words, if the employee experiences development on her job, she develops loyalty to the company who is developing her.

Meaning

They want to be involved with work that matters. They want to work for a company with a social conscience. In other words, they want their work to have a purpose. In this book, you will see a strong emphasis placed on purpose in the company, and this is why.

In reading the Deloitte research, we find that 87% of Millennials believe that 'the success of the business should be measured regarding more than financial importance.' In other words, they want to work for a company with a corporate culture that cares about more than just the bottom line on a P&L. In this way, the employee feels valued by the company, and they feel the company is valued by the community. (Remember, the community is a broader view of the customer. It includes the city and its neighborhoods as well as the people who do business with you.)

What is great about this value, is that it is a group focus rather than a "self" focus. By this I mean, my generation, (Gen X) was very focused on making a name for ourselves – having our name become famous. The next generations want to make the name of the company famous. They equate their worth (self-esteem) regarding meaning based on what the company contributes to their community and world.

Autonomy

This group likes freedom and the trust that you can let them work on their own. In fact, this group's definition of autonomy will include working in a culture that values decision-making by its employees based on the employee's value set.

In the Deloitte study, 61% of Millennials in senior management roles have 'chosen not to undertake a task at work because it went against their personal values.' By now, you are starting to see the importance of an **experience culture** to these employees.

Understand that autonomy doesn't necessarily mean "leave me alone." But it does mean "allow me the freedom to decipher and conquer through my strengths and not follow a company flow chart every time."

Efficiency

This group embraces the "how else can we do it" and hates the "we've always done it this way" mentality. So many corporate cultures today are stuck in "tradition" meaning the culture is more concerned about preserving the way we've always done it than embracing new ideas and new thinking.

The ideal CEO to a next gen does not wear a suit or a flower in the lapel. They want leaders who are beside them not in front of them. (Hear that small business owner - get out of your office!) They tend to be more entrepreneurial in spirit and value leaders who are as well.

This group values the use of technology as an efficiency tool. And when technology is inefficient (as we see so often today) they get extremely frustrated. Now, this does not mean that you have to spend millions of dollars updating all of your infrastructures, but it does point out that you will lose the **hearts and heads** of these employees if they witness inefficiencies in your company. They see it as waste, and if a culture or company will tolerate waste, then it's easy to conclude that the company will not care about the community. And the value of Meaning is torpedoed by your lack of efficiency.

Transparency

This group craves information. They want to know what's going on and they want to work for an employer who is open and honest with them even when the news is bad.

Gone are the days when a person enters a job with the plans to be there until retirement. Today's workforce is always looking for what's next. In fact, many people in jobs are on their way somewhere else. However, with the propensity of the next generations to be so mobile, it is a huge problem for companies in disruption of service and **customer experience** and loss revenue and productivity.

One of the major drivers of employee mobility (meaning switching jobs) is poor communication. Think of it this way, **communication is only effective if it is transparent** to these generations. You cannot spin or obfuscate with this employee. He will not stand for it, and she will vote with her feet and go work somewhere else.

In working with small business owners, this is always one that gives them the most heartburn. They fail to release too much detail about what's going on with the company in fear that the employee might leave. But that is simply not true.

When I had my retail stores, I posted two numbers every day as our sales targets. The first one was our cash flow number. The second one was our sales goal. In every company, the ability to cash flow (keep it afloat) is the most critical part of running a business. I have sat across the table from many entrepreneurs who were baffled because they had a P&L that said they made money last month, yet they cannot pay their bills and are about to go under.

I wanted every employee in the company to know that at a minimum, we had to hit that cash flow number. When we did, it meant payroll was fine, and their jobs would always be there (provided they delivered on experience.) It was common for one of my stores (normally closing at 6pm) to stay open late to get to that cash flow number. (I wish I could say the same for the goal.) The employees valued the transparency I gave them into the business, and they took it upon themselves to make us successful.

Now, granted, I was hitting all of the other values listed here as well, so that has a big part of why they stayed open late. But I share this story because it illustrates that employees didn't freak out and leave. They stepped up and led. Transparency is important.

Key Traits of the Next Generation

We can determine that there are some essential characteristics of the next generation employee that you should consider when designing your experience culture. While not a definitive list, these are the key traits that when you consider them, will aid in your success as a business owner today (and tomorrow.)

1. **The next generations are tech driven.**

Try asking them to punch a time clock with a time card and see how they respond. They get frustrated with employers who will not embrace technologies like cloud services, mobile POS, apps or beacons.

Communicate with them often through technology. And by this, I do not mean email. Email to the next generations is like a postcard to you or I (if you are a Gen X or Boomer that is.) Use their forms of communication. They want to know. It makes them feel valued. It's easy to do because it does not require long forms or intensive documents. Remember, this is a generation that can boil everything down into 140 characters in a Tweet.

2. They have higher expectations.

Their expectations of an employer are more demanding and higher than any other generation. If the work experience does not deliver, they will walk. They want a company that embraces technology the way they do, yet still, desire human interaction. Again, more proof that your experience culture will be paramount.

3. They have less patience.

If the expectations are not met (exceeded) then they will move on. They rarely give second chances. And when they get a poor experience, they usually share it on social media. This is true not only of their personal lives but their professional lives as well.

4. They are not as price conscious.

While other generations were all about the "deal," Gen Z tends to be more about the experience, and they are willing to pay for it. Now, this may not seem like a key trait for an employer but consider this. Today's employee "buys" his or her job from the employer. **In other words, they shop you and compare items like compensation are not at the top of their list – your culture is!**

5. They are distracted.

Most Gen Zers have more than one device they interact with during the day. And they are so tethered to those devices that they are easily distracted. They deem themselves huge multi-taskers jumping from one app to the next in a flash. But I see them more as distracted. They often miss key points in a meeting or presentation and are more difficult to communicate with.

6. They are influencers.

According to a study by Interactions, 70% of parents turn to their Gen Z kids for help in making a buying decision. Whether it is for a retail purchase or what service provider for the home or what cable company to use or what cell phone company is best, the parents ask the kids. So not only are they impacting their own buying decision, but also those of their family.

Consider that this employee is also a shopper. So how they gauge the place to work is how they gauge the pace to shop or do business with.

The Front Line is Bottom Line

The bottom line with these generations is that the front line is the bottom line. **Take care of your employee experience, and the employees will take care of the customer experience**. While compensation and benefits packages will always be important to everyone, for the next generations, corporate culture is their priority.

Study after study has shown that the millennial worker presented with similar compensation offers will choose the company with the experience culture – sometimes even if the pay is less. **They believe that a company that has an experience culture us focused on the employee experience as well as the customer experience**. And they know that when this happens, things like work-life balance and flexible schedules and leadership development will be common place.

Deloitte found that 65% of the Millennials they surveyed said 'purpose was part of the reason they chose to work at their company.' So the question at the very beginning of this book was 'are the principles of corporate culture the same today as they were in the days the first edition of <u>Culturrific</u>! was written?' And the answer is YES!!!

In fact, the truth is, **understanding the principles of corporate culture and how to drive an experience culture have become even more critical to a company's success now based on the new generation of employees.**

It's this fact that actually drove me to update and rewrite this book to be current with the changing business environment (globalization), technology and the new workforce. The bottom line for me is that companies that do not have an experience culture, better get one fast or we will be reading about them in the obituaries.

Everything Speaks

When it comes to your culture, everything speaks.

One of the exercises I do with companies is to have management complete a quick "Value Survey." I give each manager a piece of paper with 10-12 blocks on it. Within each block is a statement that relates to their business and its service. Each manager is given a role of pennies and asked to stack the pennies on the paper across each statement. They are to read each statement and then stack a pile of pennies on top of it with the number of pennies in the stack representing how important they think that particular statement is to the overall scheme of things.

The rules are simple. You must use all of the pennies in your roll, and you can distribute them any way you want. You can even leave some blocks blank. When they are done, I have them discuss their reasons behind why they stacked their pennies the way they did. The metaphor is simple. The pennies represent value. The more pennies in a stack, the more value that manager placed on that particular aspect.

The important part of the exercise is not which block wins or loses. It's that every manager's paper is different! How can we be a Culturrific! Team delivering a remarkable experience to every customer every time if the players on the team have differing values?

This is the basis for Everything Speaks. Everything speaks much more than sweating the little stuff or paying attention to detail. Attention to detail is very important, and it's not being brushed aside here, but we are trying to help you see service and experience from a different angle. When it comes to creating an experience culture, everything speaks to the customer.

Customer Speak

People make bad decisions each day in business with the right intentions. A company decides to improve its service or processes to raise the bar on customer experience and customer service. The mistake they make is when they pass service "laws" in their company that are **not** from the customer's point of view. You probably always wanted to learn a second language and now is your chance – the language of Customer Speak.

For example, you may pass an edict that all phones be answered on the first ring. You communicate, train and award this behavior to make it a part of your culture. You expend lots of money and time putting this into place. Why? Because you think it's a great way to show, you care. But what if your customers would be just as happy if the phone were answered on the third ring? How much more money does it cost you to get every phone on the first ring compared to the third? Most likely, you would need extra employees answering the phone. Who pays for this? The customer. This would be like FedEx automatically delivering every package by 10:30 a.m. the next day. They wouldn't make any big deal about it publicly. They would simply add the cost of this new "customer service" to the price of the delivery. But you are still paying for this service – a service you may not want or need.

Now, when nurturing an experience culture, it's okay to delight your customers with unexpected service. For example, in its earlier days, Zappos.com used to ship next day on orders even if the customer did not pay for it. They wanted their customers to have a unique experience by being delighted when their orders arrived much sooner than anticipated. The cost of this was absorbed by Zappos, not by the customer. But it did two things for Zappos. First, it raised the experience bar by delighting the customers with an unexpected delivery. Second, it had an impact on the employees who interacted with these delighted customers. Imagine getting a phone call from a customer to rave about your service versus complaint!

Recently, I needed to go to New York. I had a ticket but wanted to find out about flying standby on an earlier flight. I called American Airlines' 800 number and asked the woman who answered to check on flight 736 for me. She told me it was leaving on time. I said, "But I want to know how many seats are available to know whether I should risk the hour drive to the airport to fly standby." She replied, "Sir, I cannot give out that information." This was news to me and to many of you frequent flyers. I have been calling the airlines for years, and they have been telling me the "plane is half full" or "there are only three seats left on the plane." If you are attempting to fly standby, this is very valuable information. When I explained that every other time I called I got this type of information, she replied, "Sir, this phone call is being monitored, and if I don't do what I am told, then I will get marked down for it, and it will cost me money!" At least she was sincere and honest about it.

How many times have you heard the recording at the beginning of the hold message that says, "This call may be monitored for quality control and assurance?" I never actually paid attention to this before this incident. After sharing my experience with my colleagues, we decided to investigate further. Living in the DFW area, home of American Airlines, this should be fairly easy.

I contacted the corporate offices and were sent on the complimentary "transferred around the company a few times" trip (this experience is always the case in great service companies, right?). Finally, the right person got on the line and told us exactly what I wanted to hear. "This is part of our continuing efforts to provide superior customer service to our passengers on American." We then asked the magic question, "Where did you come up with this idea? Did your customers ask for it?" "Uh, no this was a decision by upper management to create a better experience on the phones for our customers." "Thank you for giving me this service," I said as I hung up the phone.

Here is a classic example of a program gone wrong. How can anyone provide superior service if they are afraid to think and act for themselves? This book is laced with the theme that you must capture the hearts and heads of your employees if you expect to develop an experience culture. **This method of "checking up on you" says one thing to the employees – "We don't trust you!"** How will you ever capture the hearts and heads of your employees if they do not feel you trust them? Poor American Airlines. Their hearts are in the right place, but their wallets aren't unless they are listening to the Customer Speak.

Customer Speak is a process of letting your customers speak to you about what they want. You should have several focus group sessions each year to find out what your customers are saying. Ask them what they wish you did differently and what they could care less if you did. Perhaps Coca-Cola would not have introduced the new Coke if they were listening to their customers. Their customers certainly spoke when it was introduced. In fact, the launch of Coke Life was directly in response to customer requests for a drink made with cane sugar. So they are learning.

There is a great myth out there that you have to spend thousands of dollars and hire slick, professional data gatherers and researchers like the ones with the clipboards in the mall. Nothing could be further from the truth. It's so easy to hold your own Customer Speak sessions in all of your locations nationwide (even globally). Place a sign at the front entrance of your business, which says:

"How would you like to get 10% off your purchase today?"

Whenever you get takers, have them complete your 10-minute personal interview with one of your front line employees. There are two wins here. First, you are gathering information that will be invaluable to you in the future as you decide what services you should and should not offer. Second, you are rewarding top performers by asking them to participate in the research. Typically, companies will hire temps to do the surveys. What kind of message does that send to the customer? Do you care what they have to say? Use the best to get the information. **It will make them feel part of the total business and not just a pair of hands and feet**.

This survey only costs you 10% off their purchase, which is probably something you have seventeen coupons and marketing gimmicks already available to do the same thing. For your business, you may use a different angle, but we have found that when you say % off a purchase, it means a lot more to the guest and you get a lot more takers than a free 2-liter bottle of New Coke.

Once you have the information, you know what to do with it. But you will need to make sure that what you heard is what they meant. Be careful not to read into what your customers are saying or put words into their mouths. Keep yourself separated from their answers. It's very natural to impose our own opinions over the ones from the customer. After all, we are customers too, right? Not of your own company, you're not. Do you buy from your company because of the way you are treated or because you get a discount? Think about it.

If you wait until you get the data back from your customers on your service, you will be reactive instead of proactive. Therefore, you will have to take a lead role in deciding and defining service and experience from the Everything Speaks philosophy.

Another idea is to tap into social media. Your customers like to talk, well at least online that is. How many pictures of dinner plates do you see a day on Facebook? How many posts on Instagram of the place the person is at? This is an instant commercial, and opinion survey all rolled into one.

Try this, put a sign on your counter or reception area that reads like this one from my shoe stores:

Tweet about your experience today *and* **get 10% off your next purchase.**

#iluvshoes

This sign was made for our Twitter customers. We also added one for Instagram and Snapchat. The idea was simple, let your Customers Speak. We got to see exactly what they said. It was easy to tell who was delighted by their experience and who was just looking for a coupon.

Notice the key word on the sign – *experience*. **We wanted the customer to talk about their experience, not just "check in" that they were in the store.** The point of all of this was to see what our Customers were saying about us – an instant focus group as we followed their friend's likes or comments.

Tours

If you have a business based on customers receiving the service or experience by visiting you (such as retail, hotel, or restaurant) and there is not a procedure for touring your business daily, then you need to start immediately. Everything speaks about looking for every little detail within your business that a customer comes in contact with and making sure it meets your service bar.

Start each morning with a walk-through of your business. Look for every little detail you can. Look high to the ceiling and low to the corners of the floors. What is your facility saying? It is speaking as well, isn't it?

Have you ever heard the adage, "If you want to know what a restaurant's kitchen is like, then check its bathrooms?" This is so true. If a restaurant cares little for the bathroom that you can see, how much care do you think they put in the cleanliness of the kitchen, which you cannot see? Next time you go to a restaurant, check the bathrooms. If they look like the ones at your local gas station, then think about eating somewhere else. Remember, the reason gas stations put the key on a small tire and lock the restroom is that they are afraid someone might break in and clean them!

If your business is conducted primarily over the phone, then try to transact business as a customer to see what it's like. How long were you on hold? What happens when you ask the tough question? How many times were you transferred? How many times did you hear "Not my department?" Or my favorite, how many times did you hear the recorded voice tell you 'your call is very important to us'? Companies that have implemented call back services are listening to Customer Speak. They are concerned about my experience on the phone with them and value my time by allowing me to get off the phone and do other things on my list while waiting for them to call me back.

And call centers, please don't try and pass off your on-hold message about your website as service to us. First, we know you are only trying to save money by making me do it myself. Second, the only time I call you is when I'm having a problem with your website. So please use your hold message to create an experience for me not antagonize me.

For example, one company we consulted with to help them launch their new product used television commercials to gain awareness. We used a professional improv comedian to make the commercials, and he was great. But then we used the same guy to create on-hold messages for the customers when they called to order. The brand extensions as terrific, but more importantly, customers commented on the hold message when they got on the line. How often does that happen? We viewed the waiting on hold time for a customer as an experience, asked them what they liked and didn't like and came up with a solution to help.

Keep in mind as you walk through on your tours, that if all you do is complain and point out the negative, then that is what your employees will focus on. Make sure you spend plenty of time congratulating and reinforcing good performance and behavior as well. That adds to the experience for your employees.

Employee Speak

Remember our discussion about the employee memos? Our discussion on communication, one of the five elements of your culture, is all about Everything Speaks. Employee Speak is different from the Customer Speak. **Employee Speak is not about what the employees are saying to you, but what you are saying to the employees!** It is one of the biggest shapers of experience in your culture.

Culture development is a marketing effort on your part. Since programming is the very root of your culture change, you must look at what you are saying to your employees with your Employee Speak. During the culture assessment, your assignment is to walk around your facility and listen to what it is saying. What do the signs on the wall look like?

For example, if you have decided to theme your culture, have you ordered all new signs that reflect the new vocabulary? If someone in your business was called the Sales Manager before and now they are called the Marketing Producer, look for everywhere that new message is being spoken:

Business cards	Newsletter
Phone list	Signs on doors
Voicemail	Caller ID on phones
Marketing pieces	Newspaper ads
Directories	What the boss calls them
Memos	Emails
How the receptionist refers to them to outside callers	

There are a lot of places to change, aren't there! "But do I have to change it all?" you are asking. Absolutely! If Everything Speaks, then everything "programs" (Culture Cycle). For every positive program you send through the cycle of the new culture you are trying to develop, it only takes one negative program (i.e. an unchanged sign on the wall) to cancel it out.

Remember the story from my first culture change attempt? Actually, since the employees' attitudes may be one of not wanting to change or of resistance, one negative program can cancel four or five positive ones! Not a healthy ratio for you!

We have seen companies spend great dollars redoing all their signage and voice mails and phone lists – pretty much everything listed above – and then hold a meeting with all the employees and talk about the Sales Manager instead of the Marketing Producer. An honest mistake, but a very costly one!

In Employee Speak, it's the little things that matter. On one trip to Disney during our research, we were told a story by one of the cast members about the Hall of Presidents. If you have never visited, it is a 25-minute show where animated wax figures of the Presidents of the United States perform on a huge stage. Each of the Presidents is represented in dramatic fashion. If you look closely enough, you will see that every stitch of clothing is authentic to the period.

Every watch is set to the correct time. But the best one was the full set of leg braces on Franklin D. Roosevelt. You may not think that is such a big deal, but FDR is sitting down, and the only way you would know he was wearing braces was to lift the pant leg. Why would anyone go to this much trouble? As a guest (their word for the customer) of Disney, you may be able to appreciate the detail in the clothing, but you would never see the braces. So why do it? Employee Speak!

No guest may ever know this story unless a cast member tells him or her. We only heard it because it was part of the tour they were giving and it illustrated a point. But every cast member at Disney knows that FDR is wearing braces. They know that because it is the only acceptable way of doing business in the Magic Kingdom. There are dozens of other examples of the Disney version of Employee Speak that have been shared with us over the years, but none so dramatic.

What about your company says attention to detail? What about your company conveys to your employees the message "Do it right the first time, every time?" Is there attention to detail in your backstage areas the way there is on your on-stage areas? If not, better add that to your list!

The Everything Speaks concept threads the message of sincerity throughout your culture. It speaks to your employees and your guests and says, "We are for real. Our culture is for real. And **our culture is a living, breathing part of our company."**

Without sincerity there is no belief, and without belief, there is no value, and without value, the wrong attitude develops, and the wrong attitude brings out negative emotions in your employees and those emotions translate into behaviors that are not constructive to your culture. Sound familiar?

Where did the word sincerity come from? It is actually from the Latin word sine, which means "without" and cera, which means "wax." During Roman times, the marketplace would be filled with artists trying to sell their creations. The sculptors, who were the most popular of the time, would stand their statues proudly on display. Many of the sculptures though would develop cracks in them. To hide these cracks, the artisans would melt the wax and cleverly fill in the cracks. Only the trained eye would know that they are getting a less-than-perfect piece. (Buyer beware started long before used cars!) So the term "sinecera" was coined to mean without wax. The statues or sculptures were checked to make sure they were sincere like we check to make sure someone is sincere.

Sincerity Check

Do a quick sincerity check on your company to check the level of commitment to your proposed values. See if any of the following fit you:

Sincerity Checklist Questions

- Does your company tout teamwork, but no one actually is assigned to a team?
- Does your company preach customer service, but more awards are given to the sales people?
- Does your company require neatness in work, but have a dirty parking lot?
- Does your company claim people are your most important asset, yet your "people" only attend one training class a year? (This one is huge for the next generations.)
- Does your company tout communication, yet you never get the whole staff (team) together at one time?
- Does your company preach customer service, but all complaints have to be handled by a manager or supervisor?
- Does your company tout empowerment, but your cashiers are required to get a signature on every check?
- Does your company claim an environment for free-thinking employees, but you have an operations manual the size of Wikipedia?
- Does your company tout customer experience, but doing so is not tied to compensation or promotion?
- Does your company claim to have a family atmosphere, but you only see the family at Christmas?
- Does your company say the front line is the bottom line, but no one in management ever actually works on the front line? (I didn't say visit. I said work.)
- Create your own quiz question. What does your company tout? And what visible and unvisible signs "speak" the opposite?

Here are some more visible signs of your culture to check:

- Does your CEO (or maybe it's you) give rah-rah motivational speeches telling all the employees of their sincere importance to the company, but could not tell you the name of anyone in the front row?
- Does your company advertise a customer satisfaction guarantee, and then management yells at an employee for honoring it?
- Does your business have more parking lot spaces reserved for staff than customers? (This is the Federal building check.)
- Do you claim to value customers, but have the line "no substitutions" on the bottom of your menu?
- Do you have lots of "Be patient with me, I'm in training" nametags? Why would anyone let someone service their customer before they are ready?
- What's it like to be on-hold with you?
- Does your website look like an entirely different company?
- Do you hire a social media intern and then blitz the airwaves for six weeks and then go silent after they are gone?
- Do you have a blog on your website with helpful articles for your customers that have not had a new article in eight months?

Everything Speaks asks you the question "Is your culture sincere? Is it without wax?" **Your new experience culture must be for you to be successful.** Make sure you pay attention to everything your new culture is saying and pay attention to everything your customer is saying. Never endeavor to build a culture you think your customer would like. Ask them. Listen to them. Never endeavor to build a culture you think your employees would like. Interview them. Their "speaking" will be the clay that you use to mold your new Culturrific! Experience. Shape it with sincerity.

The Roadmap

There are great service cultures full of great ideas, but there is only one you. Your corporate culture must be unique and personal. It's not a copy or an adaptation that you need.

It's a roadmap.

So far, you have worked on getting your "license to drive culture change." I have tried to prepare you with a foundation understanding what corporate culture is and some of the key aspects of culture that drive the change (and keep the change in place.) Now it is time to start working on your culture change.

If you are going to build an experience that is Culturrific!, you need a blueprint to guide you. I like to think of this blueprint as a roadmap. This book is laid out in steps (stops) and in the order which they should be taken. There is no perfect culture. Your culture must be unique and wholly you. The biggest mistake you can make is to try to instill someone else's culture in your business. I learned this lesson the hard way.

Keep in mind, though, that you should not initiate the culture change until you have been through this whole book and visited *all* the stops. **Remember, trying one part of the change without making sure it is connected and aligned with all the others will do more harm than good.** So read carefully and use the reflection sections at the end of each of these chapters to help keep you on track and on pace. These reflection sections will challenge you with some specific questions and remind you of the importance of people in the process.

Where I Began

My very first culture project was to create a corporate culture for a new retail concept. The investors in this project gave us clear instructions – they wanted the best experience ever. Management gave us a very generous budget, and we set out to study the great corporate cultures of America.

Of course, I started with Disney. I spent a week at Disneyland attending their training courses designed to explain what they do. I spent two weeks at DisneyWorld in Florida attending its University and gathering other research through covert operations. (You will learn more about the covert part later.) I interviewed dozens of cast members and even went through "Traditions" – Disney's version of a new hire class.

Next, I looked at McDonald's. This is a company that has long been able to turn out a product, which looks and tastes the same no matter where you buy it. That is an amazing feat! What other company can you say that about? Today, there are more and more following this model. I wanted to find McDonald's secrets since the new retail chain we were creating the culture for would be nationwide. Providing the same product everywhere consistently is the ultimate challenge for anyone in business, especially the retail industry.

There were several other organizations I studied like Southwest Airlines, Florida P&L, and Ikea furniture. I was trying to get a grip on what corporate culture was and knew our study must go beyond "like" organizations to be successful.

After months of intensive study, I decided that the best experience culture in the world was Disney's and that was who the new retail chain needed to be like. So we set out to make our retail store "Disney-esque." We even went so far as to hire a former Disney employee (cast member) to help with the writing of the training materials.

After the first two locations had been opened (within two weeks of each other), we contracted a company to survey the customers (which, of course, we called guests like Disney) to get their impressions of this new store. They telephoned several hundred guests and asked them about their experiences.

To say the comments were flattering would be an understatement. These people raved about the new store! They had never seen such a selection or had such a good time in an electronics store in their lives. The survey went something like this:

> Q.   What did you think of our new show?
> R.   It was marvelous. We had such a good time. Everyone was so friendly and helpful.

So far, so good…

> Q.   What were you shopping for?
> R.   A new television.
>
> Q.   Did you see any televisions you liked?
> R.   Oh, my yes! You have such a wonderful selection!
>
> Q.   Did you purchase a television?
> R.   Well, no. But you sure have got a great thing going there!

Ouch! Everybody loved the store, but no one was buying! At least not at the rate we anticipated. We had carried the Disney culture so far into our business that we used their vocabulary and terms like cast member instead of employee and show instead of store. We trained every cast member who worked for us that their job was not to sell but to **make it fun** for the guests and answer any and all of their questions.

We were very successful in exporting this Disney culture. We had young, vibrant, magnanimous cast members who would bounce up to you with a huge smile and answer any of your questions with style. We thought we were it. And the surveys told us we were - if we were competing with Six Flags!

One lady on a survey even said, "Oh, I didn't realize you could buy the items. I just thought it was a show!" This may seem funny now, but believe me, the CEO did not find any humor in this woman's reaction. We had a problem. We were the most entertaining place on the planet next to Disney. The only difference was the cost of admission.

You retailers and sales associates out there will get this next part. Disney's premise was different than ours. When you arrive at DisneyWorld in Florida, you have already been "closed." They asked for the order, and you gave it to them. Before you even hit the gates that first morning – before you even bought your first Mickey Mouse T-shirt or $14 ice cream cone, you have already spent big bucks. You have tickets for the family, a hotel room, and airfare, need I go on?

At our retail store, it was free to get in. We had to "close" you after you got there, not before. This was our first hard (let me emphasize the word hard here) lesson in culture. Since this first experience in 1991, I have spent the last 26 years studying corporate cultures and their impact on the business.

You will learn in the next chapter that further study on why it wasn't working revealed that Disney's "product" was different than ours. Of course, that would be a quote from an article in the "American Journal of Corporate Culture" entitled "Duh!"

Obviously, we had two different products. This statement makes sense, but on your journey to create your experience culture you will see just how much sense this statement makes.

What is the moral of this story? Simple.

DO NOT COPY SOMEONE ELSE'S CULTURE!

Your culture must be unique and personal. Although there are some principles at play, which must be present in every experience culture for it to be successful, the uniqueness of each culture is what makes it survive. Look at some of the great copy failures of today.

Southwest Airlines has been the industry leader in profitability, employee retention, and customer satisfaction. When Southwest enters a new market, their dominant presence quickly changes the way consumers in that market travel. To protect market share, the big boys have to react. (Zig Ziglar will tell you they should have responded.)

Delta created its Delta Dash service trying to follow southwest. It used the same size planes, "de-frilled" them (peanuts only) and increased the frequency of their flight offerings. Others have also made an attempt. The result? They are copying the "process" part of the Southwest culture, but not the "people" part, and their success on these flights has been very disappointing. People fly Southwest Airlines because of the culture, which includes both the people and the process. Copycat artists are always fooling themselves if they think it will work.

You must not skip any of the stops on this roadmap and must use this axiom as you go:

Borrow from the best, but use your own for the rest.

What I did learn from my experiences was Disney has some key principles that make it successful and those principles will work in any company. For example, the Disney way of training and communication includes two principles that must be in every service (experience) culture. Disney has an employee newsletter called The Eyes and Ears of Disney. This newsletter is published weekly and hits the cast member newsstands every Thursday afternoon like clockwork. The principle is not that it's weekly or it's timely (although those are good), but it's the practice of information flow within Disney. No news about Disney, which impacts the cast member, is ever given to the press until it is first told to the cast. We were told stories of Disney press conferences being delayed until the latest newsletter was out just to uphold this principle.

What a great message! "You are the most important thing to us," says Disney to their people. We want to treat you like family and never want you to read about your family in the paper before you know. This is a great lesson for all of us. How many times have you found out about a new program or project in your company by reading about it in the USA Today or seeing it on the local news? Or worse yet, having a friend ask you about it. It is a terrible feeling when you are in the dark about your company. How can your friend know what's going on before you? Happens all the time, though, doesn't it?

The Disney method of training is a solid principle as well. No new person is allowed "on-stage" without first going through Disney's "Traditions" class. This class teaches the new cast member about the experience culture of Disney. The training goes on to include about three days of on-the-job and classroom mixed instruction. Every cast member follows this Disney principle from the street sweeper up to the CEO. Everyone attends this training no matter who they are or what they do. This certainly supports the Everything Speaks philosophy! A cast member may only be working 12 hours a week for three months, but they will still get the full regimen of training.

What is the lesson here? Borrow Disney's example of training and communication. You need an employee newsletter to tell your employees what is happening in the company before the outside world does. You just don't call it "The Eyes and Ears of @hudsonhead." Make it personal, make it unique. The same would be true with the training. One of the stops on your roadmap is to create a culture training class that **must be attended by all new employees BEFORE they are allowed to report for work in their department**. But find a new name for your class besides "Traditions." Starting to get it?

You are the architect of this new culture and the driver of its bus. Your roadmap to success is listed below. A brief description is given for each stop with the details left for the coming chapters.

There are two separate parts to your culture change process. The first phase, the **Design Phase**, is reserved for your design work. This is where you map out your journey for your new experience culture. This part of your journey takes place before you even get on the bus! This is a very critical part since once you move to phase two, there is no turning back. You must make sure there are no holes in your plan before starting the engine on your culture change bus.

The second leg of your journey is the **Implementation Phase**. This is where you get behind the wheel of the bus and get the culture change started. There are more stops in this phase since the proper implementation is most critical.

The first five stops are the Design Phase of your new culture; stops seven through 12 are the Implementation Phase. Let's review them.

Design Phase

Stop 1   **Define Your Company Product**

Try to decide what it is your customers are paying for. This is not as obvious as it sounds.

Stop 2   **Cast Your Vision**

This step will set the tone for the rest of your culture-building activities because it outlines the guiding principles of your new experience culture. It includes the five basic elements of a culture and sets the emotional tone for your company.

Stop 3   **Craft Your Purpose**

There is a definite difference between a company's purpose and its vision. You'll learn about this difference in this chapter.

Stop 4   **Create Your Experience Formula**

This will be the culmination of your efforts thus far and will serve as the tool for your employees to use when it's their turn to drive.

Stop 5   **Define Your Route**

This is the stop where you plan how you will roll out your new service culture. What steps need to be taken to change: posters, signage, policies, and procedures – all of the visible and unvisible parts of your culture. **This is not an actual chapter in the book, but probably the most important stop on your journey**.

Implementation Phase

Stop 6 **Casting**

You must start with how you hire and why you hire. Turn your Human Resources Department to a Casting Department. Nothing will side-swipe you more than adding new talent into a culture change that is not aligned with the new culture.

Stop 7 **Training & Development**

Redesign your approach to training. Create and maintain a corporate university to maintain your corporate culture. Adapt new methodologies and a new culture class for your training efforts. Training is no longer a nice thing to work in when you get the time; it's part of the job description.

Stop 8 **Establishing a Learning University**

The best way to make an experience culture work is to create a functional corporate university, which models itself after a traditional university. This is an important stop that will not be fully completed for years.

Stop 9 **Awards and Recognition**

The catalysts in the culture change formulas are the tools of awards and recognition. What gets rewarded gets repeated.

Stop 10   Create a Culture Council

To keep your new experience culture alive, you must do it from the front line, not the top line. Establish a foundation for your culture to grow itself.

Stop 11   Prepare for Resistance

Whether you are a company of 10 or 100 or 10,000, you are about to change the lives of everyone of those people. You can't blame them for being afraid. Change is about fear – the fear of the unknown. Plan for it, and you will not fall prey to its powerful call.

Stop 12   Celebrate!

Do we have to tell you what to do on this stop?

(By the way, did we tell you this is a 12-step program? It's not. It's a 12-stop program.)

There are about one million things to do before you can make a successful culture shift (at least it feels that way). The purpose of this discussion is not to define them, but to give you the stops of the roadmap to make it work for your company. Each of the chapters to follow covers one of the stops. Follow them to make them work and take your time with each one. If you rush too quickly with your design and planning, it will show up in the implementation. Later in this book, I will tell you to keep the pace fast (don't let the bus drop below 55mph). This is for the implementation portion of your plan only. In the planning phase, take your time and remember to always keep these three thoughts in mind:

EXPERIENCE CULTURE

WHAT MAKES IT

UNIQUE
PERSONAL
US

?

Your Company Product

Your product is not what you are selling the customer—it's what the customer is paying for.

What is your company's product? Your first answer to this question will most likely be obvious. If you are a furniture company, then you would say your product is furniture. If you are a car dealer, then your product is an automobile. If you are a restaurant, then you will say food. If you are a non-profit, you might say homeless care. This is all fairly obvious. Why the need for a whole chapter in this book?

Two reasons. Chapter One said the reason you are taking this journey is competition. How many people did you list as your visible competition? What is their product? If they haven't read this book, then their answers will be short-sighted like the ones above. You are trying to differentiate yourselves from the rest of the world who does the same thing you do. **Therefore, you must look beyond what you are selling and start trying to understand what your customers are paying for.** And what they are paying for is very different from the wares you are hocking or the services you are providing.

The second reason also comes from Chapter One. In continuing with the theme of the visible and the unvisible, your company's product is the unvisible thing that your customers are paying for.

Herein lies the fall of many companies in today's marketplace. If you hit on a successful mix, the natural tendency is to expand your locations. The more stores or service centers you have, the more money you will make, right? Well, not necessarily.

In 1982, Tom Peters and Robert Waterman authored a book called "In Search of Excellence." This book profiled 62 companies who were considered to be the best examples of what to do in corporate America to be successful. 20 years later, of the 62 companies profiled in the book, 31 had dropped down the rankings, and 19 had dropped off the Fortune 500 list completely. And some were not even in business anymore. So you tell me. Is it really that important to know what your unvisible product is? My guess is that the people from the companies referenced above would say, yes!!! (Did you get the math that over 80% of the companies went backwards? Hmm.)

You may have the most innovative company around. Apple was like this. In the '80s, they consistently received more patents for their technology advances than Microsoft. Yet, today Microsoft owns the market. Apple is an example of a company that struggled to define to themselves and their employees what their product is. No matter how great your ideas are, your competition will soon copy them, and usually, their version is better than yours. (By the way, we recognize that Apple has made up a lot of ground and owned the market in phones, but they still are dwarfed in PCs.)

Michael Treacy and Fred Wiersema in their book, <u>The Discipline of Market Leaders</u>, talk about the importance of companies deciding on a particular discipline to follow. They describe three types of disciplines their research has uncovered. They are **customer intimacy, product leadership, and operational excellence**. Treacy and Wiersema explain that a company cannot be good in all of the three areas and expect to survive. It is too large of a task to undertake. Scattering the efforts of your people in this manner means that you may be good in a lot of things, but great at nothing. Customers today reward greatness. It's the only way to **EXCEED expectations.**

A sad example of this American philosophy is our Olympic athletes. Can you tell me who won the 200 meters Gold medal in 2016? Can you tell me who finished second or third? Can you tell us who else from the United States ran in this race? The prosecution rests. **The successful company of 2017 and beyond will be the one that is great at one thing first and good at all others second.**

What your company must be "great" at is maintaining a strong experience culture. One of the first steps is to define your product. The difference between what Treacy and Wiersema support and the thoughts here is one of focus versus product. They are concerned with a company determining their focus of strength. You are concerned with first determining your company's product. In this respect, the product must come before the focus. Your determined focus is based on what your product is.

What are some examples of products? Try to answer what you think the product is for the following companies in the graphic below.

Company   **Product**

Disney

Home Depot

Starbucks Coffee

Southwest Airlines

Your Company

As I have given this quick test to others, the responses are always the obvious— entertainment, building supplies, food, and travel services respectively. At first glance, these are some pretty intelligent answers. But answer this question. Every one of the companies listed above is considered to be a leader in their industry. Each is in an industry full of competition, both visible and unvisible. Each has reputations for being the best at what they do. People will drive further distances and put up with unusual policies (as with Southwest Airlines' no reserved seating policy) just to do business with these companies.

But these companies are leaders not because they provide the lowest price or the best food. Point of fact: You can beat anyone's price on any given day. **They are leaders because they have taken the necessary time to build a culture that nurtures their company product.**

For Disney, their product is "happiness," and if you think about it, that is exactly what they provide. For Southwest, it is "love." "Love," you say, "that's a little strange." But if you have ever flown southwest, then you understand that love is what drives the company. The employees love their jobs. The company loves their employees, and everyone loves the customer. Southwest Airlines is an excellent example of defining your product. They even have a display of that product on their planes – a heart tattooed on the side. They use this symbol as a visible sign to "program" (culture cycle) their employees and their culture.

"Now wait a minute," you say. "I never picked up the phone and called Southwest Airlines because their product is love." True, you also didn't spend half your life savings taking your family to Disney World because their product was happiness. You went because it was fun. But let's look at these two examples more closely.

DisneyWorld, for all intents and purposes, is an amusement park. Six Flags is an amusement park. King's Island is an amusement park. Knott's Berry Farm is an amusement park. In your town, there is most likely an amusement park. Why do you spend the extra money to go to DisneyWorld? What if DisneyWorld taught all of their people that their product was amusement parks or entertainment? Wouldn't Disney be successful? Yeah. Probably as successful as the local ones near you, not the Fortune 100 Company Disney is today.

Walt Disney was successful because **he knew how to get people to want to do the things that needed to be done** – the very essence of leadership. He also knew that if he asked the cast members of Disney to make their park the best amusement park in the country, then they would forever be in a losing battle with everyone else. We call this a losing battle because if you leave yourself in the same league as your competition, then you are relinquishing market share. Your sales may go up, but your share of the market or your share of the customer will most certainly go down.

So, every cast member who has come to work for Disney has been taught that his or her job is to **create happiness**. If they are the street sweeper, their job is to create happiness first, then sweep the streets. If they are the managers, their job is to create happiness first, then manage second. The ticket taker? Well, you get the idea.

The same is true with Southwest. Herb Kelleher, the former CEO of Southwest, spent his days teaching everyone in the company to spread the love. He did this by spreading it himself. I talked about capturing the hearts and heads of your employees in earlier writings. Now you can see the real power in this. As an employee, my job is to do what you tell me, and at Disney and Southwest, it is no different. The difference lies in what the employees are told. **The employees are taught the company product.**

By defining their product, both Disney and Southwest Airlines separated themselves from the competition. They used the power of unvisible to make their organizations legendary.

Home Depot's product is advice. It is what they are known for. Several years ago, I was doing a project for a tech company who wanted to know what the best retail experience was currently. We conducted focus groups around the country asking each group to tell us their favorites among a list of companies.

We had a set of consumer electronics retailers, a set of furniture stores, delivery companies, service companies and, of course, home improvement stores. We would vary the lists by the market if there were a dominant regional player that should be included. This was really important in our grocery store list.

One by one, list by list, the moderator would show pictures of the stores and ask impressions and opinions from the group. The main question was "who would you say is the best in this group?" Consistently, I mean every time, Home Depot won first place in all of the groups all over the country.

Now, these were focus groups which meant I got to sit behind the two-way glass and listen and watch as it happened. The moderator would "drill down" on the responses to understand *why* the group felt Home Depot was the best. The most common answer was "because they have those classes and seminars to teach you how to do it yourself." (They offered free advice.)

Knowing that these classes were such a big driver in Home Depot's score of first place on its group's list, I asked the moderator to dig a little more and find out what they liked about these classes. After all, it appeared we were on to something in our research and that any retail concept had to include how to seminars and classes. This is where it got interesting. In all of the groups we surveyed, **NOT ONE PERSON HAD BEEN TO A CLASS!** That's right; not one single person had attended a seminar. But they all listed that as why they liked Home Depot the best.

This experience for me is what elevated company product to the first stop on an experience culture journey. Remember, the definition of company product?

Your Company product is not what you are selling; it is what the customer is paying for.

Home Depot was ranked number one by these people. These people shopped at Home Depot for their home improvement needs. Home Depot sells lumber and hardware. And you would think that is their product. But as we see – that is NOT what the customers are paying for. They are paying for advice. They shop at Home Depot, driving by plenty of other places they could have their expectations met, to buy Home Depot's company product (and a 2x4 board.)

What is your company's product?

If you were in the coffee beverage industry like Starbucks, your product would be romance. Now, here is a neat one. Everything that Starbucks does from the roasting of the beans in their factories to the baristas behind the counter who make your coffee fresh for you when you order, to the atmosphere and design of the stores says "Coffee is a romantic experience and not just another drink." It explains why they can charge so much more for their coffee and why most of their customers pass three other coffee shops on their way to the Starbucks– because the customer is not paying for coffee, they are paying for romance!

Perhaps your product could be personalization. In today's voice mail happy automated operator marketplace, wouldn't it be nice actually to have a real person answer the phone? Even though we are in the most technologically advanced period ever, people still want to talk to people – not machines. Sorry Honda robot.

When I had my shoe stores, our product was style. (Remember the story about style consultants from Chapter One?) Everything we did had to say style. And this was a touch charge because in my stores we only carried men's sizes 14-24 and women's sizes 11-16. Now, that is a hard size range to find style, but we did it. But everything we did, we did with style. Even our return policy had to say "style" Here is the actual sign we had in our stores.

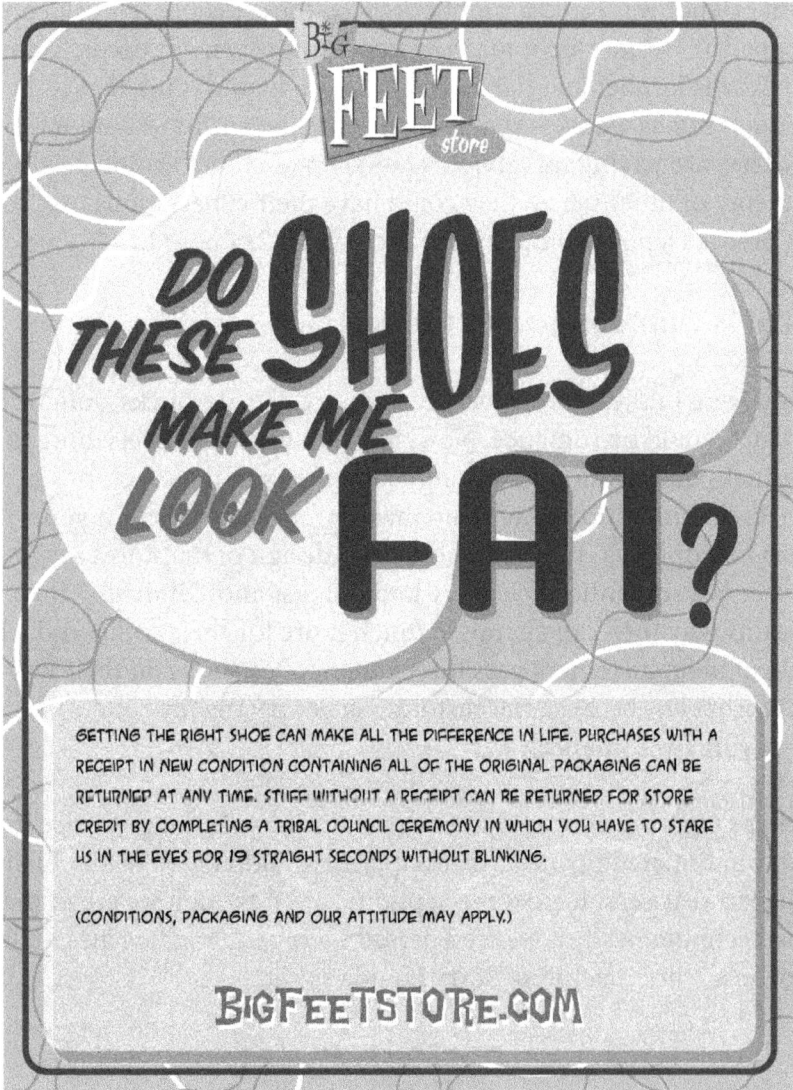

BIG FEET store

DO THESE SHOES MAKE ME LOOK FAT?

GETTING THE RIGHT SHOE CAN MAKE ALL THE DIFFERENCE IN LIFE. PURCHASES WITH A RECEIPT IN NEW CONDITION CONTAINING ALL OF THE ORIGINAL PACKAGING CAN BE RETURNED AT ANY TIME. STUFF WITHOUT A RECEIPT CAN BE RETURNED FOR STORE CREDIT BY COMPLETING A TRIBAL COUNCIL CEREMONY IN WHICH YOU HAVE TO STARE US IN THE EYES FOR 19 STRAIGHT SECONDS WITHOUT BLINKING.

(CONDITIONS, PACKAGING AND OUR ATTITUDE MAY APPLY.)

BIGFEETSTORE.COM

Another client I worked with used a product of fun. Now that would be a cool place to work. Still, another made their company product organization. And we could all use some of that in our lives.

I would love to give you a thousand more examples of company products, but unfortunately, very few are doing this! This is your chance to distance yourself from the competition. Take your time with this step. The thoughts may come to you immediately, or it may take a while. Remember this stop, as in all stops, must include people from all levels of your company. Go and define.

Reflections

What is the most important takeaway you got from this chapter?

Make a list of possible company products for your organization.

Who else in your organization can help you define your product?

Cast Your Vision

Your employees don't need a presence for the stage; they need a stage for their presence.

You set the stage. You prepare the place for your employees to flourish with their service performances providing a delightful experience to every one of your customers. There are tons of business books in print exclaiming the power of vision and purpose. **Vision is the stage.** (See quote above.)

The true defining moment of greatness for a company is when the vision translates from paper into the **hearts and the heads** of the people. It takes people to make any vision a reality. When Martin Luther King gave his famous speech many years ago, he said, "I have a dream!" What he was really saying is "I have a vision." He could see the future. He was not talking about life in his time, but life in a future time. He dedicated and sacrificed his life to helping others see this vision. Today, his vision is becoming a reality through people.

In our research, the terms "vision statement" and "mission statement" are used interchangeably by everyone. It's as if what matters is whose seminar you attended or which book you just finished reading as to which term you use for your company. But for purposes of building an experience culture, I have found that these terms represent two very different ideas with two very distinct and important purposes. And further, I have found that **the generations of today have moved beyond mission to purpose.**

What do I mean by that? Well if you recall the chapter on "Culture and The Next Generations," I made the case that employees from Generations Y (Millennials) and Generation Z want to work for companies that have a purpose. But what is the difference between vision and purpose? Is there a difference between vision, mission, and purpose?

A **vision statement** describes what your company will be like in the future. It serves as a beacon that guides management to a distant shore of possibility (very poetic.) Often, the vision is something never attained because it is disconnected from the culture, but still important in shaping your future. (This chapter talks about how to connect it and make it part of your culture through Programming.) **Example**: We strive to be the most creative company on the planet.

A **mission statement** describes how your company will do it (accomplish the vision.) It is meant for the day to day employees and is designed to give the employees purpose in the vision.
Example: We use creativity to enhance our customer's lives and our stakeholder's profits.

A **purpose statement** describes why you exist or your company's reason for being. It speaks to a plan larger than yourself or your employees. **Example**: We exist to create a better life for our customers and their families.

Your vision statement is the set of values, beliefs, and ideals you want to weave into the fabric of your culture. In the "Culture Cycle" chapter, we discussed how this "weaving" takes place. It is not enough to write down your values or beliefs on paper. It's not enough to hold a big rally and cast your vision to everyone with fancy graphics and a video. You must *program* them into your culture. But one of the key stumbling blocks for many companies is they fail to put in writing what they mean. They feel that vision is a trendy buzzword. In fact, a vision is a unique design of the future. Vision, at its core, is a strategy.

Most vision statements usually end up as verbose poetic plaques on the lobby wall or great cover story material for the company's shareholder's report. A vision is a catalyst for a company. It is a set of expectations of the future. Whereas the mission statement is about today, the vision statement is about tomorrow. The vision statement sets the emotional tone for your company. It can stir the souls of your employees and inspire them to rise to the occasion.

There are three common potholes your bus will fall into when creating your vision statement if you are not careful.

1. Never use grandiose words that are over the heads of half the employees. A vision statement can demoralize and detract from your culture as much as it can inspire and develop it.

2. A vision statement must be about values, beliefs, and behaviors. Idealistic prose will only sound frivolous to your employees. **They are looking for a reason *not* to believe as much as they are a reason to believe**.

3. It must deal with all three experience areas of your business – the employees, the customers, and the stakeholders. A stakeholder is anyone who has a stake in your business being successful. This would include vendors, suppliers, your bank, and your shareholders.

Many times, vision statements are too simplistic. They say things like "We want to be the best!" or "We want to be profitable." A business saying it wants to be profitable is like a paratrooper saying she would like her parachute to open before she gets to the ground. A vision statement is not about the obvious. It's about the visible and the unvisible aspects of your culture.

You also must be careful that the words you are using tell the meanings you are looking for. For example, when you hear the word terminal, what is the first thought that comes to your mind? For some of you, you may say train or bus, while others may say the end. Some will say a computer, and still, others will say death (this is not what we are talking about by the way.) When I wrote the word terminal, I was thinking of the little metal pieces that go on the end of wires for connecting them to power.

So, if you were to tell everyone that our new plan is terminal, some of the people would think we are getting into PCs, others would think you were going on a bus trip (little do they know), and others' hearts would drop as they think the end is near. A little melodramatic perhaps? Probably. But the point is still true. Words in a vision statement are simply that—words. It is behavior that you are looking for in your culture change.

What is the role of the vision statement? **It sets the culture cycle in motion.** It is a bond with your employees. It is the guiding principles of your organization. In the movie "Jerry McGuire," the lead character (the namesake of the title) had a revelation one evening at his company's annual meeting. He 'grew a conscious' and wrote down his thoughts for the guiding principles of the sports agent business. The result was a dramatic stir in the organization, which led to his dismissal. He left to start his own sports agency. One of the key moments of the movie is when Dorothy Boyd, an accountant, leaves the big time sports agency that fired Jerry to start the new business with him. Her reason, which she relates several times during the film, was that the new guiding principles Jerry penned 'moved her.'

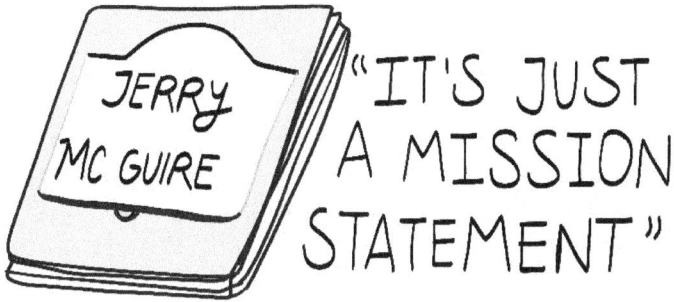

"IT'S JUST A MISSION STATEMENT"

Like Dorothy Boyd in the film, your people want to be inspired. They want to be a part of something. Your vision statement is a rallying cry of the expectations you have of anyone who comes to work for you. It is the stage for them to become great.

Creating a Vision Statement

How do you go about creating a vision statement? Good question. Actually, when you are defining your product, your vision statement, your mission (which I will use purpose) statement, and your experience formula, all of these should be done at an executive retreat away from your business. These stops are about the rebirth of your company. Now when I say executive retreat, I mean executives from all levels and departments within your business. Do not leave these important tasks to management. The largest contingency (the hourly employees) must be present and heard from during this process.

In my experiences, I have found that using "experiential" training techniques works best. However, you can get there without them. Experiential techniques require professionals and cannot be done by your own people from reading a book. Experiential is a form of training that seeks to engage the whole person in the exercise.

Each exercise is metaphor-based and can easily be related back to the workplace. The power in experiential training is that since it involves the whole person, we get to "feel" the exercise as it happens. The unlocking power of these techniques is astounding. We have never seen anything like it. Our company uses these techniques extensively.

An example of an experiential we use for this purpose is called "Square Root." It gets its name from the "squares" the participants work within during the exercise and because they are getting to the "root" of their culture – their vision's values. In this exercise, you are trying to define the six values or guiding principles that will shape your culture and will become your vision statement.

NOTE: *This exercise can ONLY be done after you have defined your product. It will greatly help your visionaries in this exercise by giving them a focal point.*

The first step is to have the group decide individually what six values they think the company should or does represent. We do this by giving them a list of ideal words to work from. This list is not the definitive, but more of a springboard to get them started. Anyone is allowed to add their own. After they decide on the six, they must debate their list with a partner in the squares. **I use six as a starting point, some cultures need just four or five, but I definitely warn against any more than eight.**

Divide the visionaries into groups of two and place them in chairs facing each other like they are in a square. Give each person six minutes (12 per square) to state their case on why they believe their values list is the best. When the groups are finished, they should have taken their lists of six and created a new list of six that they agree on.

Next, widen the square. Have the two people just debating now becomes a team, and they debate the team in the square next to them. This time each side is given 12 minutes to plead their case. At the end of the time, these squares should have agreed upon a list of six. Continue this process until you have only two squares of people. This exercise will take at least half a day with 20 people, so be prepared for a long morning.

Here is a sample list of the values words we give people to get them going:

Teamwork	Integrity	Cooperation	Family
Sincerity	Trust	Service	Love
Excellence	Creativity	Passion	Patience
Quality	Humor	Learning	Training
Courage	Pride	Fun	Respect
Innovation	Empower	Honesty	Value
Community	Team	Happiness	Care
Freedom	Recognition	Awards	Communication
Power	Self-esteem	Competition	Servant
Nurturing	Profit	Compassion	Professionalism
Catalyst	Ethical	People First	Champion

Next, you are ready to start writing your vision. This is a very important step because you are defining what your six values mean to you as a company. Also, you are dealing with the behaviors that express these values. Your vision statement is not a dictionary of terms. It is a foundation for the future. It is the guiding force to make your ordinary employees extraordinary. This process will take the rest of your day. Do not rush it! If it takes longer let it. Also, if you feel there are eight values or principles, then use eight. If you want four, then use four. However, understand that the more you use, the larger your vision statement becomes and the harder it will be to carry it through the organization. So resist the temptation to "appease" and use a larger number of values than you really need.

Give your visionaries lots of examples of great vision statements you like. Benchmark service or experience companies you admire. (Keeping in mind our working definition of experience and service here.) In other words, make a list of companies whose experiences you want to emulate – companies who provide excellent employee and customer experiences.

Contact their corporate communications department and request a copy of the mission statement and the vision statement of the company. Or better yet, just visit the company's website and check out the annual report online.

In recent years, though, we have made this a pre-work exercise for the team writing the vision statement. We ask each person to find the vision and mission statements (or purpose statements) from companies they admire and would like to emulate and bring them to the retreat to share. This approach actually works much better than you doing the work for them since they come prepared and their minds are already thinking about vision.

Key Audiences of a Vision Statement

Make sure the following are represented in your vision statement – the three areas your vision statement must address:

> **Customer** (External)
> **Employee** (Internal)
> **Stakeholder** (Both)

Your vision statement will not be complete until it contains your experience formula and your mission or purpose statement, which are the next two stops on your journey. In our off-site retreats, the vision statement is a daily activity, which does not fully come together until the last day. Even after the group blesses its finished products, they are still "trial-tested" with other groups within the company before they are put to print and considered complete.

How do you make the Vision work?

Once you have created your vision, the next question is how do you make it work? There are some simple rules to follow if you want your vision to be the powerful turbo-charged engine of your culture change bus.

- Your measurements of people must be tied to the vision statement. Levi-Strauss bases a third of its performance review ratings on behaviors consistent with their vision statement called "Aspirations." Promotions and compensation must be tied to the values and guiding principles espoused in the vision statement.
- A vision statement is only good if it is followed religiously. For your company, the vision statement is your Constitution – a very studied and modeled document. You hire to it. You train to it. You live by it.
- It must be publicized to all and included in your training. In one of my jobs, I got the company to show a video telling prospective employees what the values and vision statement were before they are even granted an interview. Extensive training on their first day discussing what "terminal" means in the vision statement follows this up.
- It must be transferred into your policies and procedures. You cannot have a policy that is inconsistent with your vision statement. You would be very surprised how often this is true!
- It must inspire the employees and touch their hearts and heads. Need we say more?

A vision is a mental picture of what tomorrow will look like. There are no time frames assigned to a vision. Goals are for quantifiable data like your sales. They have no place in your vision statement. Think of your vision statement as a picture of the future you and your employees are going to build. How much easier is it to build something if you can see the picture?

In one of the experiential training exercises we use to illustrate this point, we break the group into four teams and place them in four separate rooms. They are each given their instructions separately, but they are all given the same task – to assemble a model out of tinker toys. Team A is given full instructions and a picture of what the model is to look like. Team B is given full instructions, but no picture. Team C has to send a volunteer to another room to see the picture of the model and then run back to tell the rest of the team. They are not allowed to bring the picture with them or make any reproductions of it. Team D is given the same instructions as C.

At the end of the exercise, we debrief and discuss what happened. How did they feel doing it? What were the hurdles? You can imagine the sparks that fly when Teams B, C, and D find out that Team A had everything given to them! The metaphor? Your vision is a picture of what you are trying to build. However, just as important as the model (results), is the way you teach it to your employees (process.)

Vision is not for the executives or management – it is for every employee no matter their role.

Casting a Strong Vision

"To provide superior quality healthcare services that: PATIENTS recommend to family and friends, PHYSICIANS prefer for their patients, PURCHASERS select for their clients, EMPLOYEES are proud of, and INVESTORS seek for long-term results.

This is the vision (and mission) of Universal Health Services, Inc. This one shows the power of including all audiences in the statement. A company thrives when it pleases its customers, its employees, its partners, and its investors and Universal Health Services endeavors to do just that, according to its vision statement.

As a health care service, it specifically strives to please its patients, physicians, purchasers, employees, and investors. I also love how they emphasize each facet of the organization by capitalizing the font and making it jump out.

Here's another one for you:

"Honest Tea seeks to provide bottled tea that tastes like tea-a world of flavor freshly brewed and barely sweetened. We seek to provide better-tasting, healthier teas the way nature and their cultures of origin intended them to be. We strive for relationships with our customers, employees, suppliers, and stakeholders which are as healthy and honest as the tea we brew."

I got this one from the original business plan of Honest Tea. (Yes, the original plan.) While they have morphed to a newer version to be used as a mission statement, this original vision still stands strong. How strong? In March of 2011, Coca-Cola bought Honest Tea.

As a side note, a little company like Honest Tea getting gobbled up by a mega giant like Coca-Cola would normally have a dramatic impact on the corporate culture, but in an interview with Business Insider, Seth Goldman (founder) said "When they bought the company in 2011 they certainly had the option to say: 'Okay now we own it and we're going to cut costs and were going to shut down the office in Bethesda, and we'll run Honest Tea out of Atlanta.' That was absolutely an option that they had," Goldman said. "But because we'd been working together for three years, and working, I'd say, well together, we were each able to appreciate that there was still a lot more growth ahead for the brand and the organization, so we mutually agreed, let's keep doing what we're doing with pretty much the same structure."

So the lesson here is that Honest Tea's culture and vision attracted Coca-Cola, but Coca-Cola left them alone telling Honest Tea to thrive on its own following its vision while using its resources.

A similar story happened when Amazon bought Zappos a few years ago. The main draw for Amazon was the culture of Zappos. And Jeff Bezos told Tony Hsieh (Zappos CEO) to keep on keeping on and even encouraged Zappos to help shape the Amazon culture.

One last example for you. This is from a company called sweetgreen. sweetgreen is a restaurant that places purpose (next chapter) ahead of food.

"Our vision is to inspire healthier communities by connecting people to real food. We know that sweetgreen is a critical link between growers and consumers, and we feel a responsibility to protect the future of real food. To that end, we're committed to supporting small and mid-size growers who are farming sustainably, to creating transparency around what's in your food and where it came from, and to creating more accessibility to healthy, real food for more people. Because here at sweetgreen, the impact is not an arm of our business, it is our business, and it permeates everything we do, from what we source to who we hire and how we support local communities. We want to make an impact and leave people better than we found them, and we tailor our approach in each market to reflect the needs of the community."

I also chose this example because of their core values. I wanted you to see how elegantly the linked everything together. Hopefully, this example will inspire you to do the same. Read this from their annual report:

"These six core values embody our culture, spirit, and dedication to doing what's right. They keep us aligned and help us make decisions about everything from the food we serve to the way we design our stores.

- Win, win, win
  create solutions where the company wins; the customer wins, the community wins.
- think sustainably
  make decisions that last longer than you will.
- keep it real
  cultivate authentic food and relationships.
- add the sweet touch
  create meaningful connections every day
- make an impact
  leave people better than you found them.
- live the sweet life
  celebrate your passion and your purpose."

A terrific example that applies to us all. This book is about creating an experience culture. And this last example is amazing at embodying that very concept. And the food is just as awesome as the company. No surprise when you cast a vision based on core values that place experience (customer, community, employee, and shareholder) as the foundation.

Ready. Set. Cast.

Since your vision statement is about the future, it is up to your employees to build it. Make it easy for them. Make sure you discuss a full rollout and follow-up communication plan for not only this vision statement but also for all of the stops on your culture journey.

See what you can be. Believe what you can see. Seeing is believing and believing is seeing! Set the stage for your future success.

Reflections

What are the most important takeaways you got from this chapter?

Make a list of possible core values for your organization.

Who else in your organization can help you define your core values?

What things do you need to consider before writing your vision statement?

Craft Your Purpose

Your company's vision statement communicates the guiding principles of your culture, but your company's purpose statement communicates your product.

Is there a difference between a mission statement and a vision statement? Absolutely! The vision statement described in the last chapter was designed to help ALL the stakeholders know the purpose of your company. The vision encompasses the big picture ideals of your company. It sets forth the guiding principles of your culture. But how much does a verbose Shakespearean piece of paper mean to the hourly person working 30 - 40 hours each week punching the clock? Nada. (Hopefully, your new vision is not one of these or I have failed you in the last chapter.)

Not only do these front-line people rarely care about your vision, they probably will never see your vision, and you don't need them to, not if you have a strong mission statement. In the best world, the vision statement would be clearly communicated to everyone in the company, from the part- timer to the CEO, but we have to be realistic. What is the mindset of the average person working for you? Hands and Feet. That's it.

Sure **your goal is to capture their hearts and their heads**, but this will not happen overnight, and the reality for a good percentage of your employees is that it will never happen. The vision statement is the foundation on which your culture is built. The audience for it is everyone, but the ones who need it tattooed to their hearts is management. They are the ones who get to "program" your vision into the culture.

When I was working in retail, one of the standard training practices I employed was to send the new salespeople out to shop the competition incognito. When they came back, each one would share his or her experiences. It was amazing the stories these new salespeople would bring back. They would tell of the "lower" end of the service scale. They would describe the failing businesses they visited, obviously on their last legs. We would let them continue a few minutes having their fun picking on the competition; then we would stop the discussion with this question "If these guys are so bad, why are they still in business?"

The question would bring silence to the room. People would venture a guess, but very seldom did anyone ever get close. The answer was simple, yet it evaded them. "Why are they still in business? **Because the same people you were making fun of work for us to!**" Wow! What a powerful statement.

"No. Couldn't be." These were their responses. But ah yes, it is true! No matter how great an effort you put forth building the perfect Culturrific! Experience team, there will always be those on your team who will bring you down. If all of the great people worked at the same place, then there would be no such thing as competition. There would only be one winner. But that's not the way it works.

The moral of this story is you must develop processes that are clear and simple for your employees to understand and easy for you to hold them accountable too. There is a great number (about two-thirds of your workforce) who will be a challenge for you during and even after your culture change process. You must plan for this large number to be successful. In the next two chapters, we will discuss the steps necessary to do this. Keep in mind that what we are prescribing is a way to speak to the front-line service providers who are not at your company to make a career. An interesting survey would be to poll your workforce and ask, "Who is here because they want a career? And who is here for the money while you're on your way to somewhere else?"

Especially in a company full of part-timers, you will see a trend to get the paycheck, but not the payoff. How many people do you have in school? Are they studying to get their degree in your company? Of course, not. They are studying to make themselves prepared for the next step in their lives, and that next step will not include you or your company. This is fine. We are not criticizing these people at all. In fact, if you have a company with strong ethics and moral values in your vision, wouldn't it be nice to know that you had a positive impact helping to shape someone's character through your culture? It would be great if integrity was one of your key values and the employee going to school to become a lawyer learned it from you. (We need more lawyers with integrity.)

But the fact remains that if you are not working for a company as a career, then you probably are not using more than your hands and feet. I could write several books on how to capture these people, but you are better served adding a dimension to your experience culture to address these employees in a positive, constructive way. You must equip them to be great experience providers for your company. **They may only be with you for a short while, but they can have a tremendous impact on the future of your company.**

Mission or Purpose

In the Vision chapter, we gave the definitions of vision, mission, and purpose as it relates to your culture change journey and business strategy. Mission focuses on what to do and purpose focuses on what to be. So while there is a clear definition line drawn here, after years of working with companies on their mission statements, I have come to the conclusion that purpose is more powerful than mission.

First, the shift in the value structure of the generations from Gen X and Baby Boomers to Millennials and Gen Z has placed more emphasis on **purpose** than mission. Since the majority of workers are from these next generations, it bears to reason that the majority of income will be in these generations. (Not regarding net worth or wealth, but in spending.)

Customers today choose companies who have a clear purpose in making the community they serve a better place to live and exist. They reward companies who care for employees and give the employees a purpose with their business. In a 2017 study of consumer shopping behavior, 75% of next gen shoppers said they would choose a local business with a clear purpose over a national chain. Essentially these respondents are saying they are looking for purpose and will choose those companies EVEN OVER PRICE! (Meaning they will spend more to do business with a company with purpose.)

Second, no matter how I may define the terms mission and purpose here in this book, **the general public will always consider mission about the company and purpose about the community.** I even tried a culture change where we used all three – vison, mission, and purpose. But it became convoluted and confusing to employees. Therefore, I have switched to using purpose in a new way. **I now believe in a mission that is about purpose.**

So, for the rest of this chapter, you will read the word purpose versus mission. For some of you, you may still want to use the terms interchangeably, and I don't think that's all bad. Just be sure that even if you continue to use the term mission statement that it is grounded in purpose.

What's in a Purpose Statement?

So after all that discussion, what is a proper purpose statement anyway? For your company, it is one that meets the following criteria:

1. **No more than 10-15 total words in length.** If you want to achieve success with this, it must be something the employee can memorize and repeat when asked. Any longer than this makes it very hard, and when most people think something is too hard,

they avoid it. Management can memorize hundreds of words, but they get the vision statement.

2. **It must be tied to your product**. The first stop is to define what it is that you are really selling – your product. This product MUST be in the purpose statement.

3. **It must be printed everywhere for reinforcement to the employees**. Many companies print it on the back of the badges an employee needs for access. Another company I worked with on their culture change printed it on the paycheck stubs.

As told earlier, Disney's product is happiness. This is what people are paying for when they visit the Magic Kingdom. Their mission (purpose) statement is:

"We create happiness."

Simple. Straightforward. Powerful. Through this simple statement, Disney reinforces to every cast member in the company that his or her role is to create happiness, not sweep up trash, not take tickets or sell souvenirs. It is to create happiness, the very thing distinguishing Disney from all others.

Red Robin Restaurants, International's product is "happy guests." Their mission (purpose) statement (which by the way could be found printed on the napkins on the table when they launched it) is:

"We create happy guests."

Try to create a simple statement like the ones Disney or Red Robin uses. Imagine the power of having everyone in the company working towards "happiness" or "love," as is the case with Southwest Airlines. We are not concerned that every value and every belief be communicated in the purpose statement. The vision statement is for that. **The purpose statement is to communicate your product.**

The Purpose Statement Rules

(Yes, there is a double meaning here.)

What are some rules or guidelines to follow when creating your purpose statement for your experience culture?

1. Never use words that are open-ended. Words such as "best" are hard to define since everyone has a different opinion of "best."
2. It must not be a separate idea or concept from your external marketing, vision, and experience formula. Many times companies will introduce a whole new thought at this point. This is a mistake. The military is successful at taking people from all different educational, social, and economic levels and bonding them into a common purpose. They do this by sending the message over and over and over. They stray from verbose messages and repeat the same themes everywhere, increasing the repetition to the trainee. You should do the same thing within your organization.
3. Make it part of everything you do. It should be in front of every employee all of the time.
4. People will believe what they are told through programming. You know this is true. If you are told enough times that you cannot change your company's culture, eventually you will believe it. But on the other hand, if you tell your employees enough times what their purpose is, eventually they will believe it as well! This will only take effect after many, many months of programming.

Is there power in a short purpose statement? Of course, especially if it is about your company's product. Continental Airlines had a short, one sentence purpose statement.

"To be recognized as the Best Airline in the Industry by our
Customers, Employees, and Shareholders."

And it worked for them. After being named "Best airline on flights
greater than one hour" by J.D. Power and Associates for multiple
years in a row, they merged with United Airlines to create one of the
largest travel companies on the planet. United stated that it was
Continental's dedication to purpose that made the merger attractive
to them.

And what about this one:

"A computer on every desk and in every home."

Can you guess who owns this one? Who else, but the billionaire boys
club Microsoft. (I always wondered if their purpose statement was to
rule the world.)

Here is a real forward thinking company:

"Build the best product, cause no unnecessary harm, use business to
inspire and implement solutions to the environmental crisis."

This is Patagonia. They are an apparel and gear manufacturer for the
outdoors lifestyle. Patagonia's purpose statement combines both the
values that bring them success (building safe, high-quality products)
and the values that contribute to a better world (help the
environment). Patagonia believes "a love of wild and beautiful places
demands participation in the fight to save them." As part of its
purpose, they donate employee time and at least 1% of their sales to
hundreds of grassroots environmental groups around the world.

**If your business wants a similar focus on growing your
revenue *and* giving back, think about talking about both the
benefit you bring to customers and the value you want to bring to
a greater cause (the community) in your purpose statement.**

Here's another great one:

"Warby Parker was founded with a rebellious spirit and a lofty objective; to offer designer eyewear at a revolutionary price while leading the way for socially-conscious businesses."

I love this one because of its kitschy nature – which is the essence of its culture. I also like this one (although a little long) because it is equal parts purpose and mission and vision all in one. And it resonates with employees as well as customers.

One more:

> "To maximize profits to shareholders through products and services that enrich people's lives."

Did you guess this one? This statement is a little vague and doesn't necessarily fit our model of a great one, but I have to give balance to this discussion. This is Nike. Nike seems to be doing okay with this statement. The amazing thing about this company is that it has carried the one-line philosophy over to the advertising with the "Just Do It" campaign. It was not until this campaign (which came about as a joke between a couple of the advertising people on the Nike project) was launched that Nike achieved superstar status.

Nike is an excellent example of a company that has used marketing to make itself great. It has not only marketed to the public, but also to its own employees successfully. Nike management constantly reinforces this mission statement. However, the amazing thing is— Nike doesn't even make shoes! The shoes are all built for them by contractors. But the employees of Nike are just as proud to sell the shoes as if they had personally sewn them. This is an example of the power of purpose. Nike supports the second point above about tying your purpose statement to your marketing.

What is the purpose statement of your company? Can you recite it? "Uh, uh no." or "Oh, I know this one. Give me a minute. It's something about…" Sound familiar?

A mission statement that is not known by the people (placed on their hearts and heads) is about as useful as a parachute on the first bounce.

We thought it would be intriguing to find out how many people really know their company's mission statement. Over the past years, asking this question of people I come in contact with in all parts of my life has become a norm for me. It's very hard to serve me food in a restaurant or rent me a car or check me into a hotel without being asked, "What is your company's mission statement?"

I even took it so far as to call companies out of the yellow pages (yes, the actual yellow pages. I got one delivered to my house, and before I dumped it into the recycle bin, I thought, let's have some fun.) I spent a couple of afternoons asking the people I got on the phone if they knew their company's mission statement. (This was the fun part because at times I posed as a radio deejay or as a braniac professor from Harvard. It was very hard to get people to take me seriously without the ploys!)

Well, throughout this investigative research process, I have come to this conclusion.

More people know the mission statement of Star Trek than knowing their own company's mission statement!

(Now there's a quote for you.) It's true! I started asking people what the Star Trek mission statement was and they knew it! Oh, please! Don't sit there reading and try to pretend you are not "boldly going where no man (or woman) has gone before!" You probably struggled with the first question, "What is your company's mission statement?" but had no trouble with the Star Trek mission. That's okay if you're Gene Roddenberry, but it really doesn't do a whole lot for the profitability or service of your company.

Why do people know the Star Trek mission statement? The main reason people know the Star Trek mission versus their company's is that they had actually heard the Star Trek one — many times. Our experiences showed employees are never even told the mission statement of the company let alone their mission as a part of the company. **Is it any wonder that people will give you only their hands and feet at work?** If all I do is wait tables at Red Robin restaurants, then what are my chances that I will make a "happy guest"—which is their product?

Red Robin International is a great example of a company that tied its mission statement to its marketing. On the front of every napkin they printed this mission statement: "We create happy guests." Definitely a page out of the Disney book. Steve Udhus was the Vice President of Operations for Red Robin when they launched their culture change. When interviewed about it, he said, "There is no set culture that you can go out and buy. But there is a blueprint (roadmap) that you can follow that builds and molds your culture successfully. We studied and benchmarked the best to discover the blueprint, but we had to do the building ourselves. Our culture is unique, distinctive, and of service." We have found that it works and every employee of Red Robin knows that their job is to create happy guests, whatever it takes."

To see the real power of this mission statement (Disney's as well) you must look to the word "create" in the statement. The definition of create is "to produce or cause to exist." **This means that the employee must produce happy guests. It will not happen on its own**. The employee must create them. It's not about the food or the height of the drop on the roller coaster. Rather, it's about the interaction with and the behaviors of the employees that creates their cultures.

These are some powerful thoughts to remember when creating your company's new purpose statement. It is the behavior of the employees that creates the happiness, not the policies, procedures or marketing gimmicks. And how do you influence or change the behavior of a culture? Correct! You send positive, reinforcing programming through the culture change cycle and you will achieve success.

You Are the Author of Your Fate

Through the years, I have seen a mistake made when it comes to the crafting of the vision and purpose statements – **they are not written by the employees; they are written by an ad agency**. While consulting your marketing team for help with wording, never let them write it for you. Let me give you three reasons this is a bad idea:

1. They are disconnected from the process. They have not been in the room and digested all that you have.
2. They focus on the customer only. You need to focus on all three audiences – customer, employee, and stakeholder.
3. They think the message inside is different than the message outside. While this has been the predominate belief in marketing for decades, the example companies I am using in this book all buck that convention. They unabashedly share their vision and purpose with the public – the same one they share with their employees and their shareholders.

You must write these statements as a team. Think of your marketing people as proofreaders or copy editors (like I have for this book.) These people never change my points or emphasis, but help me relate my message in the most compelling way. And they correct my typos as well.

Your purpose statement is the programming that needs to happen every day. It is the key to changing your culture's behavior. Do not let it lose its purpose or power by "wording" it down. Tie it to your product and then program, program, program! As great as Star Trek is, it means nothing to the experience culture of your company. Make it so!

Reflections

What are the most important takeaways you got from this chapter?

Make a list of possible words to use in your purpose statement.

Who else in your organization can help you define your purpose?

What things do you need to consider before writing your purpose statement?

Create Your Experience Formula

The front line is the bottom line. This is where the experience happens.

Chip Bell and Ron Zemke in their book <u>Managing Knock Your Socks Off Service</u> shared some of their research about having a "formula" to enhance service. They found:

- If you do not have a definition of what good service means – your chances of getting high marks from your customers are about 3 in 10.
- If you have a very general definition – your chances of getting high marks from your customers improves to about 50-50.
- If you have a detailed definition (or formula) of what good service means – defined in the context of the customer and the company—then your chances of getting high marks from your customers are close to 90 percent!

You can take those last comments and replace the word service with experience because it works the same way. As you move forward with your new experience culture, more and more people will become involved with the process. Eventually, the process takes over, and you are always evolving to a better, more productive and efficient culture.

To let your new experience culture govern itself, you must develop and establish an experience formula. What is an experience formula? Let's start with a couple of examples.

Disney's formula is:

$$
\begin{array}{c}
\text{Quality Cast Experience} \\
+ \\
\text{Quality Guest Experience} \\
+ \\
\text{Quality Business Practices} \\
= \\
\text{Future Growth}
\end{array}
$$

As you can see, Disney has taken into account all the players involved in their experience (they refer to it as service) formula. Let's take a look at another one. We are all very familiar with Sears. Everyone reading this book has a story about themselves or their parents shopping at Sears.

For years, the Sears name and its bountiful catalogue were trademarks of American culture. People used to buy the Sears catalogue just to keep it on the coffee table as a sign of prosperity and good taste.

As with all companies, eventually, the playing field changed on Sears. Its corporate culture was choking to death one of the greatest retailers ever built. We see this example over and over when a company's culture is built on its way of doing business. This way was built for a time in the past. The rules change. Competition changes. The day always comes when your company's way of doing business will have to evolve and change for it to survive. **The survival rates are directly proportional to the success of the regeneration of the corporate culture to be in line with the company strategies for doing business.**

We have cited a company whose culture had kept them from keeping up with the change in competition. Sears was fast becoming another one. Sears had to act, and the actions they had to take would be painful.

The CEO at the time, Arthur Martinez (since gone), came well equipped to reconstruct (or reengineer to be trendy) the Sears culture. After dumping the catalogue operations and other companies such as the Discover Card, Sears was ready for the culture change portion of their plan.

To guide the employees of Sears through to the new culture, Martinez crafted the Sears service formula:

> Make Sears   A Compelling Place to Work
> +
> A Compelling Place to Shop
> +
> A Compelling Place to Invest

Sears, like Disney, had taken all three major parts of the equation and married them together. Both of these companies have learned that to marry yourself to only one part of the equation will mean disaster in the competitive world of today.

Now you may be reading this last part on Sears and be thinking, "Matt is crazy! Sears is all but done." Exactly. I wanted to include an example of a good experience formula not executed on by the culture. You see, often, the story is "read this example and then the happily ever after ending." I wish every culture change that I was involved with had a happily ever after ending, but they haven't.

It goes to show you that ALL of the ideas in this book (stops on your journey) have to be addressed and aligned, or this simply will not work. A beautiful graphic with a compelling experience formula will not change your culture by itself. You need all parts firing on all cylinders – which is why this is so hard. Remember the story about JC Penney from before?

Doing part of the work will not bring about change. It will bring about turmoil.

Finding your discipline or product, whether it is operational, customer intimacy or product excellence is much easier than having your newly-defined discipline come alive in your culture. The larger issue I see today is to many companies working in "silos" – meaning each department functions as its own kingdom. So compensation is not connected to awards and recognition, which is not connected to training which is not connected to performance reviews which is not connected to career growth.

Balance is essential for sustained market success. It creates win-win-win results for everyone: customers, employees, and shareholders. Imbalance, however, puts businesses into a bad cycle that ultimately leads to bankruptcy.

What is the balance? The three-part experience formula. You must consider the impact of every decision you make on ALL THREE parts of your business. What are the three parts?

Employees
Customers
Stakeholders*

* A stakeholder is anyone who has a stake in your company doing well. This includes shareholders, as well as suppliers, distributors, etc.

Disney and Sears are both saying the same thing in their experience formulas. They are just phrasing it differently to fit their culture, which is exactly what they must do. Imagine going into a Sears store and hearing someone refer to himself or herself as a cast member? Wouldn't feel right, would it?

However you phrase your experience formula, it must include all three parts. One note here. **When I refer to the customer in this formula think of it in the larger context as well – community.** When we consider that the new generations are about purpose and impact on the community (neighborhood, city, etc.), then you can see why this larger view of customer makes sense.

So, what is an experience formula actually saying? And what is its purpose? Good questions.

What is an Experience Formula?

First, an experience formula works like this. Whenever you are faced with any decision, you run it through your experience formula. The experience formula works like a filter. It filters out any potentially erred decisions BEFORE they happen. Let's say you have a new operational process that you want to introduce in your company. You must first ask yourself:

How does it affect the employees?
How does it affect the customer?
How does it affect the business?

If you get a negative response to any of these three, then you simply do not do it! More companies have shot themselves in the foot because they have only paid attention to one part of the experience formula or they make decisions with a two-thirds majority rule. The two-thirds majority rule may work in Congress but will get you in big trouble in a service-oriented business. (Incidentally, it is not by accident that I use Congress here since the two-thirds rule really doesn't work for them either.)

I once bought an air pump at a Target store in Fort Worth, Texas. Now, keep in mind I like Target, and they get a lot of my family's money, but this story will show that even the good ones can make mistakes.

Anyway, the air pump I got was the super-deluxe-blow-the-tire-of-a-monster-truck-up-in-four-seconds-version with color racing stripes on the side. A real man's air pump if you know what I mean. This pump was amazing. It could do everything…except pumping up my basketball, which is why I bought it in the first place! So I had to return it.

When I arrived at the Target store, I took my place in the line at the "Guest Services" counter. (Everything speaks in action.) The gentleman in front of me was returning a defective video he had purchased three days prior. He had his receipt so it should be no big deal right? One would think so.

Two girls were working behind the counter, and when the man in front of me placed the video on the counter the girl looked at it and said "Oh, great! One of these!" holding it up to show her partner. "I hate the way we have to do these now. Do you know where that new log book is?" she asked her friend. "Not me" the friend answered, "look in the back." The girl went to the back, and like your favorite Wile E. Coyote cartoon, a loud series of bangs ensued. Emerging from the back, the girl held up her trophy, the elusive log book, used to process returns of videos.

During this process, the gentleman in front of me did what we would all do in his situation. He turned to the people in line behind him and apologized like it was his fault! Have you ever done this?

The girl continued her disapproving comments to her fellow team member (another Target culture vocabulary word) while she processed the man's return. People behind me started to switch lines. They didn't want to be responsible for messing up this girl's day. No way!

Imagine how this customer, excuse me, guest felt. Imagine how the Target team member felt as she was processing it. Imagine how the other guests in line, like me, felt. What do you think the impact was on the business? Exactly. In all likelihood, that Target team member cost her team money and future business that day. We know that it cost Target, the gentleman with the defective product's business. He expressed this to everyone in line after he got his return processed.

Now, this is not an indictment of Target. Target has been very successful at achieving change to a service culture, but today was not their day. Today was a result of someone not following the experience formula philosophy.

Let's examine this incident. The new process for returns was probably a wise decision for the business because it kept the cost of the return down which in turn kept the cost of the newer goods down. (i.e. Target does not have to inflate pricing to recoup lost income.) Okay, so we passed one question. Obviously, this was a good policy for the guest or customer because they receive the benefits of lower costs and, with Target giving 5% of their profit back to the communities they serve, the customer benefit is even greater. So, we pass question two. But what about question three? How does it impact the employee? Here is where Target got bit.

Somewhere in the implementation of this new process, Target forgot to consider what the implication would be on the employee who had to carry out this new procedure. This is where we see many companies trip up. They fail to recognize the impact their decisions have on the employee.

If you are customer-cantered, then you better think about who services your customer as much as you think about the customer!

Here was an example of a policy designed to help the customer that backfired. It failed to consider the service provider. **Your best service is only as good as your best service provider.** One little-known fact is that Disney spends more money on litigation each year than most any other company. Now, who would want to sue Mickey Mouse?

The Purpose of the Experience Formula

We could dig deeper and find that Target did do its homework and this new policy was no more cumbersome and difficult to perform than the old way, so it passed question three as well. Here comes the second part of your experience formula – the implementation of your decisions.

Your experience formula guides your decisions to make sure you only make ones that will positively impact your profitability; but, it also serves as a reminder for the implementation of these new decisions once they have been made.

In our Target example, we may have encountered a team member who was never properly trained on the new procedure and therefore was resistant to it. When you are answering the question, "How does it impact the employees?" don't forget that how you communicate and implement the decision must be answered as well.

Once the new business decision has been made, then run your implementation process through the three questions again. Email has become the policy writer of today. The tragedy is that possibly 75% of your service force does not have email. Email is left for management who says, "Well, we sent them an email!" What would the answer be to the three questions if you said, "We are going to send out a notice on this new policy via email?" Let's hope that it would not make it through.

Hold on a minute here; this is not fair. Sometimes we have to make tough decisions. And sometimes those tough decisions are going to be painful for the employees. They just have to learn to live with it. If you believe this, then know this. Not only will they have to learn to live with it, but so will your customers and ultimately so will you! Anytime you go against the experience formula; you are fighting a losing battle.

The experience formula also guides your outward decisions as well. Make sure that you tie yourself and your company only to those decisions that follow the same experience formula concept that you do. If you use an outside advertising agency, for example, make sure they are on board. Not just in spirit, but in culture. It is always the tendency of the ad guys to champion the customer. Sometimes the greatest deals for the customer are the worst deal for the employees.

We can remember many grand opening specials produced by the marketing gurus of consumer electronics retailers that ended up in disaster because the idea was not run through the formula. For example, they would advertise a 42" LCD television for $199. That is a hot price. It would have been nice if they had printed the fact there were only 20 available at this advertised price! This would have saved about a dozen lives of front line service providers who were torn apart by angry customers when they found out there weren't any $199 televisions left.

Management inside your organization can also use the experience formula as a battle cry or slogan for its efforts. The biggest fear of management is when it has to tell the employees that, "We are not going to do it your way; we are going to do it our way!" This evokes controversy, and no one wants to deal with this.

Instead, what if everyone knew of your experience formula? Then, management could capture the hearts and heads of the employees by walking them through the formula as the basis for the decision. This makes great training and builds tremendous teamwork. Plus, it eliminates the personalities involved that often cloud the issue. It's not the outspoken employee Madeline who is against the new idea, it is the experience formula – it's the culture!

Do not let management ever use any part of your experience formula or mission or purpose as a scapegoat for doing things their way. Your managers' way better be the stated written way of your four power tools of culture—the vision, your purpose statement, your product, and your experience formula.

In the later parts of this book, wI will introduce you to the Culture Council. You will see how this experience formula becomes a great tool for employees as they make decisions. Employees will always tend to come up with ideas or suggestions that are a little grandiose. They may be great for the employee and great for the customer, but the business will lose money and cannot afford it. An experience formula keeps you on track.

Empowerment and the Experience Formula

How could we write a book about service and experience and not include a discussion on empowerment? There is probably some law about this somewhere! Empowerment is one of the most talked about, preached about, and written about topics today in companies of all sizes. Most empowerment initiatives by companies fail. Do you know why?

We pose this question to many of our training classes and the usual responses are:

- The person acts empowered and then gets beat up when they make a mistake.

- Management really doesn't trust the employee fully enough to let go.
- The employees were not trained sufficiently.
- Management likes control and feels that if you want it done right…

All of these are great responses and can be argued as the correct one. But there is one answer that is more correct than these, and it is VERY rare that anyone gets it. The number one reason empowerment fails?

Because people have to want to be empowered!

You cannot give something to someone that they do not want! When the decision to be empowered was made, did we consult the hourly front line about it? Chances are 99% that they were not asked.

Management ran their decision through only two parts of the experience formula – the customer and the business and got positive responses for each. But what about the third element – the employee? How will empowerment affect them?

An empowerment initiative is an issue that needs a formula to be successful. Remember, the answer to the three parts of the formula also takes into account how the decision is carried out. Getting a positive answer to all three is only half the equation. You must also develop a plan of implementation that takes into account all three parts of the experience formula as well!

Empowerment is a good thing and is necessary for a Culturrific! Team. However, the way you implement it makes all the difference. There are tones in every chapter relating to this point. Trust is what makes empowerment go. **Trust is only achieved when you have captured the hearts and heads of your employees**. When you have done this, they will want to take the power.

Before we finish, here are some more examples of experience formulas:

Engaging Employee Experience

+

Delightful Community Experience

+

Effective Business Strategies

=

Bliss

This is my experience formula from my chain of shoe stores. Notice how I took the customer and expanded to the community as shared earlier. In this way, we thought of our customers and our community (city) the same. Plus, since we had no investors (except mom and dad) there was not a need for a stakeholder component.

Our brand was rather kitschy in messaging which reflected our culture thus the use of the word "bliss" in the experience formula. If we hit all the targets, then naturally my life as a small business owner would be full of bliss.

Best Place to Serve

+

Best Place to Be Served

+

Best Business Practices

=

Success

This formula we created for one of our clients. I always liked the way it communicated that the brand and company was all about service. With the best place to be served, you actually could say that they were focused on the employee experience and the customer experience.

The experience formula is the visible part of your culture, which reminds everyone in your organization what you stand for and it equips every person in your organization to be able to make decisions for you. The only way you can ensure they make the right decisions is by creating a service formula for everyone to follow.

From the front line employee down to the CEO, whenever there is a decision to be made, it must be passed through the filter that is your experience formula. **If you get a negative response to any of the three questions, then you simply do not do it.** It's like the management at Red Robin Restaurants always says in its employee meetings, "Is the decision we're making being 'of service?' "— a shortened version of its experience formula.

Reflections

What are the most important takeaways you got from this chapter?

Make a list of possible ideas of your experience formula.

Who else in your organization can help you craft your experience formula?

What things do you need to consider before writing your experience formula?

Casting

If "All the World's a stage," then why are all of the understudies working for us?

Have you ever felt this way before? Who hasn't? "It's so hard to find good people these days" is the favorite saying around Keurig. We're not going to spend any time in this book lecturing how you must have good people to build an experience culture – you already know that. But sometimes what we know and what we do differ...greatly!

While working with a Fortune 500 retailer, I was asked to help develop a training program to reduce sexual harassment incidents in the company. The number of incidents had been steadily climbing, and so had the legal bills. Management decided to train everyone on sexual harassment. As I sat at the table and listened to all of the opinions jostling about from the lawyers, HR people, and so on, I became very confused. We were going to create a video to teach people not to harass sexually, I thought? Seriously?

Finally, I jumped in and asked what I thought was a rather astute question. Why are we spending money training people not to sexually harass someone when they already know not to do it? The glares I got. "Are you not paying attention?" they said. "I believe I am," I replied. "The part I'm confused about is why we don't spend our money on hiring the right people in the first place? If they are someone who will sexually harass, find out in the beginning. We test for drugs. We check for integrity and tendency to steal, why not check their background and personality on this subject?"

Well, needless to say, I was not invited back to the next meeting. Why? The answer is simple. The culture in place told the people that there is only one way to do things – fix what you have control over and leave everything else alone. To attack this problem, we didn't need a video to say stop harassing people, we needed a better hiring process, which meant getting into someone else's world. Sterling Jewelers (the parent company of Kay and Jared Jewelers) is in the middle of a class action lawsuit on sexual harassment that has thousands of employees involved. Do you think it's the training or the culture?

When you are building a Culturrific! Experience for your employees, the first rule is

The example above, while dramatic, is indicative of most companies. They want to have an experience culture, but they are not willing to go all the way with it. The first place to start building your new culture is in your Human Resources (Talent Management/ Acquisition) department. If you do not put the practices into place there first, then every day that you make progress in building your new culture will be offset by the hiring of someone who does not fit.

The proper selection and hiring of new employees in an experience culture goes beyond testing and resumes to a term called "casting." Casting is the process of placing the right people in the right role in your company. You can hire anyone, but if you are casting someone, you are thinking about the people side of the culture. **All companies are relatively good at the process side of culture change; it's the people side that tends to baffles them.**

You are switching from the paradigm of "filling holes on a job requisition" to "casting someone as if you were a producer of a Broadway play or a Hollywood film." How important is it to put the right talent in the lead parts? All you need to do to answer that question is look at the exorbitant amounts of money today's actors get paid. Putting the wrong person in a role is devastating to the movie's financial success. What does your experience formula say?

We seriously doubt that the HR people of today have this kind of urgent mentality when they are hiring. A former HR Director for a Fortune 50 company once said to me, "When is the last time a company ever fired someone for making a bad hiring decision?" The answer is probably never. Why? Because they are hiring people, not casting them.

First, Recast Your Human Resources Department

The first step is to get your Human Resources team on board with its new role. They are now "casting directors" responsible for the success of your service performance. They must act, think, and behave this way. This is difficult because HR school teaches these people to be overly professional and cautious. This new role for them may be intimidating at first. Be patient, but be firm.

Probably the most famous casting building in America is on Interstate 4 in Orlando. There stands a beautiful, ornate building used by Disney to hire its new employees. If you have done any research at all to this point, you know that Disney has one of the strongest experience cultures in the world today. Its culture is based on the theme of being more than an amusement park, but literally being an extension of the movies and characters Disney has created throughout the years. They do this with the Everything Speaks philosophy by making sure the message is communicated to the prospective employee right down to the doorknobs of the buildings, which are shaped like the characters from Alice in Wonderland.

There are a lot of things in the Disney casting process that are brought about by necessity due to the sheer volumes of people who apply; but, there are three key principles Disney practices, which can be used in any business.

1. Everyone is interviewed when he or she shows up. There are no signs that say come back on Thursday from 2 to 4 p.m. Disney casting is open regular hours and has plenty of cast members ready to make sure they can accommodate you when you arrive. Why is this important? Think about the message this sends someone when they apply. It says, "You are important to us," "You and your time are valuable" "We care about you," and lastly, "Isn't this the type of company you would like to work for?" Wow! Those are some powerful statements.

2. Front line cast members interview the people. Although some regular cast members are working in the casting building for Disney, many are temporarily assigned cast members from their regular jobs. These cast members are well trained in interviewing before they are turned loose.

Obviously, we do not have to support the wisdom of having front-line people help in the hiring process. It's amazing that we involve everyone in the review process in companies (through 360-degree feedback), but we seldom, if ever, involve them in the hiring process. Who knows better what a person needs to do the job effectively than the people who do it every day?

If you have a position inside your company called "Recruiter," regenerate (reengineer) it into something else. It is no wonder so many service companies have such high turnover when they leave the hiring decision to someone who has no involvement in the service process. Remember to train the front line person to do the interview properly. We are not suggesting that you throw out all of the lessons you have learned in the past from your hiring practices. We are also not suggesting that this front line person be the only interview.

Although, if you look at the amount of training given to the managers who are currently doing the hiring, does this point really matter? If you are more comfortable, then have your second interview done by someone more seasoned.

3.   Everyone is introduced to the Disney culture and expectations immediately. One of the great ideas we picked up from Disney was the addition of a video to the interviewing process. Many companies have videos to tell the company history or explain the benefits, but few spend the dollars on the cultural aspects of the business.

We have reviewed dozens of "recruiting videos" from companies that really belong in the orientation process once you are hired. As a matter of fact, I'm convinced someone higher up got the great idea to combine the videos into one and save some money. If you make this mistake, you are missing the point. Whether you use a video or paper screening process, you must weed out the people who will not fit your culture up front. Not during the interview – BEFORE IT! (You'll hear more about this topic later.)

It's not just a hiring practice created by the "casting director" that's important here. Disney could use any rules and set any policies and still be able to staff all its theme parks two times over. Disney receives about 16,000 unsolicited resumes a year in Orlando alone from people who want to work for them. It goes without saying that they can hire whoever they want, right? Not necessarily. The reason these three casting principles are in place is because of the Disney culture. Remember its service formula from the last chapter? Provide A Quality Cast Experience + A Quality Guest Experience + Quality Business Practices = Future Growth.

Using this formula, what do the three casting principles imply? First, the principles are about providing the prospective cast members with a happy, enjoyable experience. Why? Because until you are hired at Disney, you are its guest! So Disney is providing a Quality Guest Experience. Then, at the end of the interview process, Disney will tender an offer right there on the spot. What does this say? Quality Cast Experience. As a new cast member, you can expect to be treated this way—always.

The point here is that the people who run Disney casting are not looking for the easiest way to hire new people or the quickest. They ran every one of their policies, procedures, and practices through their formula. If they got a negative answer to any part or if any part was in question, then they changed it or did not do it. Is this really necessary? You tell us. Of the 16,000 resumes referenced, 50% of them are from people who have college degrees, some well beyond bachelors. Why would these people want to leave their well-paying jobs to work for Disney for minimum wage selling popcorn to ungrateful kids? Here's another one for you. Are people lining up at your door to be hired? Is there a waiting list for your company? Could there be? Absolutely!

When you are hiring, the following rule should apply:

HIRE SOMEONE
WHO FITS YOUR
CULTURE

What does this mean? Simply put, the majority of hiring decisions are made by looking over someone's background and experience. The "more years of experience" or the "more degreed they are" the better employee they will make –at least this is what the traditional approach to hiring tells us. Now, do not call legal and say that this book says don't hire old people. That's simply not true!

Experience is an excellent teacher, and if the person comes from a compatible culture, this experience will be very valuable to your company. What I am trying to illustrate here is that casting is about looking beyond the background of the individual and into who the person is and what they stand for. Are their values in line with your vision statement? Do they come from a company with similar values?

Does this sound familiar? "You are going to love this guy. He has 20 years in customer service." Hey, was that your recruiter who said that? I thought we reengineered them already? You have heard the phrase many times and the next time you hear it – be scared! More important than the 20 years of experience is the culture in which this person has been working. If you recall our definitions and explanations of culture, you understand that the person becomes a product of the culture, not the other way around. Therefore, this person may be very experienced and has produced some impressive results for his or her past companies, but in what cultural environment? In other words, at what costs? **The old company culture comes with him or her and depending on the position in the company; it will influence yours.**

When I had my retail stores, I used to hire all of my cashiers from drive-thru lines at fast food restaurants. (When you meet me, you will see that I do a lot of recruiting.) The principle was simple. If I encountered a person in the drive thru lane that was magnanimous and genuine and concerned about my experience, then that was someone I wanted on my team.

Think about it. When you go through the drive-thru lane, you normally get your order repeated back to you; your change made and a thank you. But when you encounter someone who makes it an experience, it stands out to you. Recently, I was at McDonalds' and when I got to the window to get y order, the gentleman opened the window and sang "da dah dah da dah, you're getting McDonalds!" Now, you need to refer to their music for their jingle to get that reference, but I was blown away.

You see, McDonalds trains every employee the same way to do the exact same thing. They teach customer service and friendliness to every employee, but this guy was different. He had something special, and it was not the training. His core values (people, service, experience) matched mine for my business which makes him the perfect hire – he fit the culture.

Remember this – you can train product knowledge. But you cannot train core values. Those come with the employee already. By hiring people from fast food restaurants, I was not getting anyone with knowledge about shoes for my stores. But I could teach them that. It's the customer experience that matters, and they delivered every customer every time.

In one of my past lives, I had a job where everyone in the field was required to wear polo shirts and khaki shorts. Anytime someone from corporate went into the field; they were required to wear the uniform (or "costume" as we called it).

Side Note: This was a problem for us. My division was part of a larger company with many brands, and the "corporate" people wanted suits since that's what we always wore. I got in trouble more than once showing up to a meeting in my uniform.

I kept a picture of myself on the wall dressed this way. During any interview, I would always refer to the picture and ask the applicant "What if I said you had to come to work dressed like that every day?" For the most part, people were fine with it—after all, it was shorts! But every now and then, someone would look it over and turn to me and say, "No, I wouldn't want to dress like that guy." Bingo. This guy won't fit the culture. This was hard sometimes, too, because this may be someone I was impressed with on paper and came highly recommended. By the way, my first clue should be that they rarely realized the picture was me!

Imagine the negative influence someone can have on what you are trying to build. Perhaps this potential manager got great results on paper but had the highest turnover in her department because the culture did not value people. Many companies believe the bottom line rules, and they do whatever it takes to make that bottom line. For you, there is a new rule:

The front line is the bottom line. Treat your people the way you want them to treat your customers.

This means that, to take care of that valuable front line, you have to be very careful not to put any stress or bad influence into the mix. The principle of casting is about protecting your culture and the people within it. An influence like this can be very damaging. You have total control over this situation. When you err on a casting decision, err on the side of culture and fit, not professional experience.

When Steve Jobs, the founder of Apple Computer, left the company, it started into a tailspin. The marketplace was changing dramatically, and the Apple culture was slow to react. The Board of Apple brought in a "quick change" artist by the name of Gil Amelio to serve as CEO. Amelio's job was to kick-start the failing Apple back to its prominent days. Gil Amelio had a good history of being "experienced" at this task.

Amelio met with much resistance as he implemented his new policies and procedures. He was a brilliant and capable man, but there was just one thing wrong with the person who did this casting – Gil Amelio did not fit the Apple culture. Amelio came from National Semiconductor. The two cultures clashed, to say the least, and Amelio was caught in the middle. Even by his own admission, Gil Amelio has talked about the power of the Apple culture and the difficulties of introducing his methods. It's not that Amelio could not be a CEO, it was simply that Apple broke the first principle of casting – hire someone who fits your culture. Gil Amelio really never had a chance. And Apple paid the price. Bring back Steve Jobs and…

When do you hire?

We consulted with a hotel once about its selection process, and it was determined that the current employment ads really did not send the message of the culture. So, we decided to redesign the ads, but the HR Director stopped the discussion when she said, "But we don't have any open positions right now." BUZZZZZZ. Wrong answer. You ALWAYS have open positions. In an experience culture, you need the best and brightest on the front lines and managing your future all the time. There will always be weak links in your service-profit chain—no matter how good you are. **The trouble with most companies is they wait until they have an opening called – "someone quit" – before they run an ad**. If this is your practice, you might as well make this the header on your classified ad in the Sunday paper.

The longer management has to wait for a body; the more likely the company is to put a body in that spot literally. You need someone who can be empowered and think on his or her own, not just stand there like a Donald Trump cardboard cutout. As a matter of fact, if this is your company's current culture, my recommendation would be to purchase two or three of these life-size cutouts and stand them at the counter. This certainly would do much less damage to your service-profit chain than the live body would, and their benefits package is much smaller. (Not to mention their girth.)

Earlier I described Disney's process of creating a hiring video. First, it's important to note that this information was not discovered in an interview with key Disney cast members or management. I (and a couple of others) went to Florida and applied for a job, like anyone else, to see how they did it—sort of a secret shopper mentality.

First, we were required to watch a 10-minute video as a group. In this video, they covered their culture, their expectations, and some of their rules. For example, one of Disney's policies at the time was no facial hair on men and no hair below the bottom of the collar. This is explained in the video.

What is the point? If you explain what the culture is like and what the rules are up front, you can weed out a lot of potential "non-culture fits" in the process. At the end of the video, everyone is given a chance to leave with his ponytail still intact gracefully.

This accomplishes two things. First, it allows someone to say, "I don't want to be here" with little or no embarrassment. Second, it frees up the interviewers' time to spend more quality time with each applicant. Either way, you are saying to the person (who may be your customer someday) we value you.

We implemented this process at one of my jobs. It was amazing, the number of people who would walk out at the end of the video when they heard what they were going to have to wear, how they had to conduct themselves, and what the culture was all about. It was equally amazing the number of people who thought we either weren't serious or it did not apply to them. When you use the video, make it a habit of asking them this interview question first – "What did you think of the video?" Again, the purpose of the video is to let the applicant know what he or she is getting himself or herself into.

Now, maybe you do not have rules about hair length and color, but there are many expectations you do have—like transportation or the ability to work odd shifts, etc. Make sure your video incorporates the following:

> A Day in the Life of an Employee of Your Company
> Dress Code and other HR stuff
> Your Cultural Theme
> Cultural Vocabulary
> Your Product (HINT: this would be the one from earlier chapter)
> Your Purpose
> Your Experience Formula

Hire Creativity Creatively

Another very good idea in casting is to test for expression and creativity. An essential attribute of any service or experience culture employee is creativity. They will be faced with many decisions that will require them to draw on their creativity. Currently, if your company is like most, the only creativity expressed is in the excuses for not showing up to work or for poor performance! In a traditional non-service themed culture, tough decisions and creativity are left to the manager. This will not work in your culture. **It will not yield a remarkable experience every customer every time.**

How do you test for creativity? In every interview situation, we have ever examined, there is always a time when the applicant is asked to "wait here" until the interviewer is ready. This is typically in a lobby or waiting room. Try this. When the applicant has completed his or her paperwork, have them wait in your "creative room." This is a room with tables of construction paper, glue, markers, crayons and various other craft items. Hang a sign on the wall, or place one on the table that says, "Show us your creativity."

While the candidate is waiting, they are to make a small crafty item that expresses themselves at that moment. Be sure to place some examples from past applicants on the walls to give them a starting point. By the way, try to use examples from people you actually hired. It would be embarrassing to have a killer display and have someone ask, "Who made that one?" and your answer is "That guy, we didn't hire him."

Not everyone will take the hint and make something for you. There is no problem in being more "leading" in this process by having the person who puts them in the creative room to instruct them to make a craft. What will this activity tell us?

First, those who choose not to make anything are probably not the ones you want. Many will find this activity childish or immature. In other words, beneath them. You are building a Culturrific! Experience team. The key word of which is experience! If someone feels it is beneath them to do this little thing, how beneath them is it to do the menial tasks that need to get done? They are people who hire people to do that for them. They are also not for you.

C. William Pollard, the former chairman of ServiceMaster Corporation, tells a story in his book, The Soul of the Firm, about his first week on the job. He was hired as the vice president of the company but was required to spend his first week cleaning a hospital's floors, hallways, and bathrooms (including the toilets.) He recalled being very indignant about the whole process but went through it anyway. The chairman of ServiceMaster at the time Bill was hired, Ken Hansen, had one belief – no one could lead in his company unless they knew who and what they were leading. (Talk about positive programming!) Completing this first assignment would teach Bill servant leadership and what service was really all about. What a message this sent to Bill Pollard about the culture of ServiceMaster. How many people would be willing to pay this price to work for your company? We all talk about the importance of knowing the job, but we rarely practice it. The creative craft idea is one way to find out in the interview.

Granted, many of the crafts you get would not even make it on the refrigerator at mom's house, but that is not what you are searching for here. Unless you are trying to hire someone to redecorate the office, the only thing you care about is the attempt and the experience.

Ask the applicants to bring their crafts with them to the interview and let them explain their meanings. This makes a great conversational piece to break the ice. You also can combine the video room and the creative room into one if you are short on space, but make sure they do not start their craft until AFTER they have viewed the video. If you recall the importance of folklore in your culture, you have already made the connection between these crafts and some of the hallways in your company office. Nothing makes for better folklore than a tour down the hallways looking at the crafts of the past and seeing who did them.

The Unvisible Parts of Casting

So far we have discussed the basics of casting, but what other areas do we need to look at? In keeping with our theme of everything Speaks—everything.

- **What about your employment application?** Does it look like everyone else's? Does it communicate your culture and who you are? Through our studies, we have seen applications from a half-page long to five pages double-sided. The smallest, of course, being the placemat on our tray table at McDonald's.
- **What about your lobby?** What posters or pictures are on the wall? Do you have pictures from the culture or generic pictures or better yet, the pictures that came with the frame? (That last one is not a joke, I actually found this during one of our audits.) How long do you make them wait past the set appointment time? For every minute they wait, you are sending the message that people and their time are not important here. For many companies, it is considered a "good" practice to make the applicant wait for a while. After about thirty minutes, the

interviewer comes strolling out like the king or queen of the small country called Human Resources. And then they speak, "I'm so sorry you had to wait, but you see there are so many other things in my kingdom that are more important than you." Yeah, you are going to get some real go-getters this way. Probably, these kings and queens think they will convey the message that this is a very important company to work for. We have two words for that. Who cares? It is not about what the company can do for the employee; it's about what the employee can do for your customer and your culture.

- **What about your casting process?** Does someone have to wait to get interviewed? Will they feel valued by you during the process? Are they being treated as if they were your best customers?
- **What about your interview questions?** What are you asking prospective employees? It is very common among retail companies to pose scenario-type questions to the customer service applicants. These scenario questions are hypothetical situations the interviewer makes up to see how the applicant would deal with it.

I call this practice of behavior-based interviewing the "screen test." For example, "You have a customer who is returning a computer for the second time claiming it is defective. You know that you are out of stock on the model and it would take about a week to get a new one. What would you do?" In this situation, obviously, we are looking for the answer "substitute them another comparable model to take care of them immediately."

Or how about, "You have a customer on the phone who has several charges on her bill she feels are incorrect, and this is the fourth time she has called to get it fixed." This is a tough one because you cannot see the customer's face and the customer cannot see yours. It has often been said of me that I have a great face for radio or the telephone. Who cares what my face looks like? It's how well I can handle your customer that matters.

The question here is, "Why do we only pose this scenario to the customer service applicant? Why not to the other people as well? Bill Fromme and Les Schlesinger in their book, <u>The Real Heroes of American Business and not a CEO Among Them</u>, wrote how everyone in the organization must be focused on customer service. The front line and the support line. Ask the same questions to the warehouse guy that you do to the customer service agent. This book goes on to support this thought with case studies of some of the best customer service people in America. This is sound advice from people who know.

In my many years of training and consulting, I have done tons of videos. I have even produced and directed a dozen national television commercials. When we would cast for the roles in these videos and commercials, we would have the prospective actors or actresses complete a screen test where they would read some of the lines for the part on camera. One of the things we always considered during this process was the way they handled themselves off camera.

In other words, what did our receptionist think of them? Were they rude or arrogant when they came in? Or were they polite and courteous? After all, these were actors so they should be able to play the role very convincingly. But when they were in the waiting room, they were *themselves*, and we would have our receptionist give us her list of who she liked at the end of the day and why.

We took this one step further and started having the cameraman, and our assistant ranks them as well. They were not concerned with how well these people acted; just how well they carried themselves otherwise. The crew always wanted actors that would be easy to deal with and who could blame them.

Recently, I was sitting in the lobby of a prospective client. (We tend to screen test our clients as well.) These people were wonderful on the phone and spoke of their undying commitment to their customer and their people. While we were waiting, a well-dressed man walked in with his wife and asked the receptionist if he could speak with the same man we were waiting to see. The receptionist called him on the phone and then told the man she was sorry, but no one was able to see him. The man inquired again offering that he was from out of town prospecting for a new position and would only be in town that day. The receptionist called our hero again and this time came back with a "Mr. Alexander is very busy and said that if you had a resume to leave it."

Why is this story here? Because the company we were visiting was a job search agency, which placed relocating talent. These people, who told us how people-oriented they were and how much they believed in the cause, were not even courteous enough to greet the gentlemen in person. They did not have to spend time with him. They simply could have shaken his hand, explained their situation and then invited him to leave his resume with the promise to follow up later. All of this would have taken three minutes. Besides, what was so pressing? They were already 15 minutes late for us! (This whole being late thing seems to be a real issue in this book, doesn't it?) Needless to say, I declined to work with this group. The driver of their bus was a little scary. He had a great talk, but no walk.

You should adopt this same practice of screen testing at your company. Using the screen test approach, check with all of the people the applicants come in contact with. **You may be very impressed with them during the interview, but if they are acting, you need to know it.**

Attracting Millennials and Gen Zers to a Baby Boomer workforce can be challenging. But while their culture is different from older generations, they share many positive values. Current trends show that the next generations are interested in many things beyond money—they value time with family, will not sacrifice their quality of life for a career, and are very team-oriented (see Culture & the Next Generations). These characteristics could help explain why interviews have gone up in retail specifically—according to the recruiting software firm **jobvite**, the average retail hire is up against 35 other candidates. This seems to be because Millennials tend to take more interviews and talk to more potential employers before committing, and this can be great news for your company.

Here are 9 ideas to help you recruit and cast the best Millennial and Gen Z talent:

1 **Personalize the Experience**. No different than the shopping habits of Millennials who want an **experience in a retail store**, the applicant is looking for the same thing. It makes sense that they consider the interview and hiring process as a preview into what life would be like working in your company. For example, conduct the interview outside our office or backroom. Find out if they like coffee or yogurt or diet coke and buy them one while interviewing. Make sure you do more listening than talking. This is the hardest one for managers, but it speaks volumes to the candidate. They need to be heard.

2 **Pay Referral Bonuses.** More people were hired in 2016 from referrals than newspapers or signs in the front window. Tell your employees (and customers) that you will pay a bonus for a referral you hire. Make it worth it though. Giving someone a gift card for a free latte will not motivate anyone. In my stores, we gave $300 in store credit for referrals. Now, that is a big number to an employee or customer, but since they are buying merchandise with it, it honestly cost me half based on my gross margins. Now that's a win-win for sure.

3   **Be on Social Media**. Post your job openings on social media. That is where Millennials and Gen Z are searching these days. And be creative when you do. Share the referral bonus for example. Remember, it's not about your followers on social media, it's about theirs. They will retweet or share your post on Instagram with their personal network, and you are getting it sent to thousands.

4   **Team Interview**. First, you will want to expand your interviewers in the process — meaning, have more than yourself conduct an interview. In fact, I recommend having the peers be involved in the interview process. There are a few reasons for this technique. First, it displays to your employees that you **value their opinion** and that they are part of a team and not just an employee; they are vested. Second, it models for the potential candidate how you do business. When they see that you include the employees in the process, they know that they will get the same treatment when they work for you. And third, often times, an employee can "translate" for you with a candidate.

For example, you talk about your company's **customer experience** and give an example story, but your story or example may not resonate. When a peer tells a story, it's related to their level. Consider that I am 52 years old and when I talk to a 21-year-old candidate, it doesn't sound the same as when another 21-year-old talks to them. Something I get frustrated with, but just have to get over. Finally, ultimately you will be asking your employees, to train, mentor and nurture the new employee. So, if they helped choose the employee, they have a vested interest in their success.

5   **Shadow**. Allow the candidate to shadow another employee to see exactly what the job entails. You are casting someone for a role, and this will show the prospective employee exactly what the part is they are being asked to play. This one tip alone can save you a lot of frustration. No matter how well you explain the role, no one will ever truly understand until they experience it. One note, in some states (like California) this idea might be frowned upon as it is a fine line between the person working and observing. But keep in mind, they are just observing nothing more.

6   **Use Behavioral Questions**. Many of your candidates will have little work experience, so it's hard to know if they are the right fit for you. First, remember, you always **hire people who fit your culture**. But if you use situational (behavioral) questions, you can gauge whether or not this candidate can perform at the level you need them too. For example, "tell me about a time you had great service experience from a business. What was that like?" or "Tell me about a time you had a bad experience, how did that make you feel? What did you do about it?" Obviously, the best scenario is to pose situational questions about them at work. For example, "tell me about a time you had a frustrated customer, what did you do?" But you have to consider that much of the Millennial and especially Gen Z workforce has limited work experience. But they all have life experiences that can tell you a ton about how they are "wired."

Here are some more good question examples: Tell me about the best service experience you ever had? Where would I find you on the weekends? Who are your heroes? Why? (Credit for this one goes to Bob Fromme. His belief and ours is that people try to emulate their heroes. The qualities that make this person their hero will be qualities they admire and try to practice themselves.) Who was the most influential person in your life? Why? What is great customer service to you? How do you keep yourself motivated when you feel down? Tell me a funny story about you that happened at work.

7   **Share What the Candidate Cares About.** In most interviews that I observe, it is a ton of talking to the manager about what they expect or like. But, the candidate never says much. First, this model for the candidate that life working for you is about you and not them. Millennials and Gen Zers are about work environments that focus on them.

So, instead of focusing on things about your company that you think make you unique, focus on the things younger candidates are looking for in an employer. Remember the first core value the next gen wants from an employer? Development. The younger generations want to work for a company that will develop them and help them grow. So talk about your commitment to training and development and what that looks like at your company.

8   **Talk Benefits Not Pay**. Millennials, especially, are not paycheck focused like we have seen in previous groups. They want more. First, by benefits, we are not talking about insurance or sick pay. We're talking about the extra benefits of working with your company. For example, in my stores, I let the employees make the schedule and give to me to approve. They got to choose their shifts and hours they wanted which created space for them to have a strong work-life balance.

Share the "perks" of working for you that include the intangibles that you may have left out in the past. Show them the rewards and awards you give out for great performance and great customer experience. Recognition is a big deal to Millennials and Gen Zers.

9   **Be Desirable**. One of the most significant things you can do as an employer is to be desirable to the candidates. Does your company have a social conscience? Are you a part of the fabric of the community or do you just take from it? Are you in the news for your good works or your gimmicks (or issues)? If not, you will have a hard time attracting millennial talent. The truth is, if you cannot answer yes to these last few questions, you are going to have a hard time staying in business. Keep in mind Millennials make up the majority of the workforce now, which means they will be the majority of the customers.

For years, the number one reason an employee left a job to work somewhere else was, lack of recognition. The next generations are changing that. **They leave a job for lack of engagement**. Does the job engage them? Is the company engaged in the community? Does the company help the employee be a better person through the development and transparent communication? 60% of all Millennials leave retail within the first three years—not for money or career advancement—but because they want more from an employer. And that more starts with casting and the way you recruit and interview.

Here are 4 Tips to help improve your interviewing practices:

1   **Focus on behavior**. Too many interviews focus on what people "think" and not what they do. As a man, I know it is proper (and gentlemanly) to open the door for a lady. But do I actually go around the car and open her door? So I would tell you it is the right thing to do and you might infer from that answer that I would do it.

Just as with your coaching of an employee, you have to **focus on behavior and not attitude** or opinions. Try to understand how they would respond to a customer. Focus on what they will do, by understanding what they have done, and that means ignoring the job title from the previous employer and focusing on the character and "wiring" of the candidate.

2   **Ask their Opinion.** Often times during an interview, we tell the candidate about our core values as a company. But rather than "tell" the employee, turn the tables and ask them what they think it means. For example, rather than explain what integrity means as one of your values, ask the candidate what they think it means.

It is very easy for someone to "parrot" back thoughts you are sharing and agree with them. But when you ask me my thoughts without sharing your own first, you are getting raw and pure responses. In fact, use this technique a lot during the interview. Listen for themes and consistencies among their responses. You will start to get a true glimpse into the candidate's character if you do.

3   **Ask the Frustration Question.** This is one of my favorites. Ask the candidate what frustrates them in a situation related to your company. Or ask them what frustrates them about a job they had in the past. Knowing what "pushes their buttons" gives a peek into their wiring. For example, if they share a frustration story about messy offices, then you know they value organization.

But if they share a story about an employee they didn't like, then you are hearing about their personal pet peeves or frustrations and not what frustrates them. If the key to success today is customer experience (which it is) then you want an employee whose frustrations deal with these issues.

4   **Study the Non-verbal.** Probably the one area interviewers ignore the most is the non-verbal communication of a candidate. This is most often because the interviewer is doing most of the talking versus the candidate (which is a terrible mistake in itself.) If you are practicing good interviewing techniques, then the candidate is doing the majority of the talking. And as they are talking, you get to study their nonverbal communication.

Do they truly believe what they are saying? Their body language can tell you that. For example, when you ask them a question, as they respond is their posture confident and assertive or are they fidgety, struggling for an answer. You need confident employees. It is the only way to provide an exceptional customer experience. And the interview is where you can truly see this in action.

While these techniques are targeting the Millennial or Gen Z candidate, the truth is they apply to any candidate. Remember, **hire people who fit your culture**. And that may not mean they have the most experience. You can always train product knowledge, but you cannot train someone to be magnanimous or genuine or compassionate. These are qualities you need to hire. And these are qualities you can see in a candidate if you use the right techniques.

Performer Profiles

Who does your manager hire? Someone who is like himself, right? This is the time-honored practice of millions of companies. But if our principle is to **hire someone who fits the culture**, then having a structured profile of who you are looking for and what their talents are is very important.

You must provide a resource to your person doing the hiring that outlines the knowledge, skills, attitudes, and habits that fit your culture. Make sure these profiles are not too wordy, but not too generic. My least favorite "attribute" listed on every job description is self-starter. What does that mean? Who knows, but everyone wants them! Oh, yeah. Don't forget the ever-popular motivated individual.

These performer profiles will take on more shape in the "Create a Learning University" chapter. For now, suffice it to say, you must be very careful with your new culture and creating hiring profiles will help.

Recasting for profitability

One of the key ideas of casting is to recast your performers every now and then. By recasting, I mean placing them in a different role within your organization. There are several benefits from this process.

- **Lowered turnover.** When an employee feels stuck in a spot with no upward mobility, they tend to start looking outside the company for their next move. If you build this culture correctly, this will be a huge problem for you because no one will ever leave your company and there will not be enough management jobs to go around. You could take the path of some who have created positions for people just to keep them like "Director of Salad Bar" in your restaurant, but this will soon do you in.

  This is probably why everyone went out rushing to try Michael Hammer's reengineering techniques several years ago. They found themselves with too many salad bar managers – one for romaine, one for iceberg, one for potato salad and so on. If people are not challenged, they will find someplace that does it for them. This should be no surprise to you once you've seen the tie between culture and self-esteem.

- **Increased profits**. This one goes without saying. The less hiring you have to do, the more money you can put to the bottom line. The more cross-trained people you have, the better you can recover when someone calls in sick. Having a cross-trained organization means the customer never has to suffer when the players (employees) change.

- **Develops a bench**. In major league baseball, the talent you see at the ballpark during the game is a result of years of development in the minor leagues. If you recast your employees, you will have a bench ready to step into an empty spot. It keeps you from hiring poor service providers out of need as we shared above. A manufacturer in Arizona postponed for six weeks the firing of 30 employees caught using or selling marijuana and cocaine. They were afraid of what would happen to production if they did. They obviously had no bench ready. Hopefully, your company has not had to use drug users to do your service while you get new ones.

- **Raises the experience bar**. The more experienced employees are in different roles within the company, the better service they can provide which leads to a better experience for the customer. Carl Sewell, the owner of the Sewell car dealerships in Dallas and Fort Worth, Texas and the author of Customers for Life, says companies should eliminate their customer complaint departments because in a service company it is the responsibility of every employee to handle complaints. Cross training and recasting provide for this. This is a great benefit to the customer since they do not have to go through 17 different people to get satisfaction.

- **Increases employee morale**. Increased job knowledge has been linked to increased job performance. And a job well done has been linked to self-esteem. The better we feel about ourselves, the better we will perform. There is no doubt about it.

There are three rules for recasting you must follow to make it work.

1. **Always post every opening for all employees to see.** Never allow an exclusive or insider job listing. You know the type we're talking about— where only corporate office employees see what's available, but not the field employees. Also, be careful not to let your managers create new positions like assistant to the assistant manager's assistant. This is an example of your culture's communication.

2. **Always make training part of the recast.** In the next chapter, we will discuss the role of training in your new experience culture. In that chapter, we will propose a set training plan (or degree plan as you will read) for each position. An employee should not be eligible for recasting until they have completed the training plan. This is a hard one, and your managers will try to shortcut this all the time. Watch them!

3. **Make sure that each recasting has at least 12 to 18 months in between**. Your employees may pick it up quicker than this, but most of the training of a job is through experience. They may know the basics, but the more scenarios they can get exposed to, the more powerful they will be for you. Also, the time required makes the feeling of accomplishment that much greater.

The role of casting versus hiring is simple. You are trying to build a Culturrific! Team to provide a remarkable experience to every customer every time. And to do so, you need to prepare the employees to be creative and onstage at all times. They must be actors playing a part for the customer, whether that part is putting away merchandise or solving a problem over the phone or handling the accounting. Traditional hiring will not work for you. You must examine your current practices carefully and replace them with the thoughts in this chapter.

Every bad casting decision you make will cost you. As you start to build your new experience culture, the most important thing you can do is to **hire people who fit your culture.** You are not looking for the best or most experienced talent. You are looking for the best and most experienced talent to fit your culture.

Challenge the notion that "there's just not enough good people out there." **And whatever you do, NEVER hire someone to fill a spot. It will cost you more than a number on your annual turnover report. It could cost you your culture!**

Reflections

What are the most important takeaways you got from this chapter?

Consider your current hiring practices. What needs to change to make you a "casting" company?

Who else in your organization needs to read this?

Training & Development

Knowledge is potential not power. It's what we do with the knowledge that makes it powerful.

cul|ture (kul'cher), n., v.,**-tured, -tur|ing. –n.** development of the intellect through training or education.

Remember that definition? The success of building a Culturrific! Team to deliver a Culturrific! Experience is directly proportional to the quality of the training program you design and maintains for your company. In the past, we have tried the traditional techniques and methodologies. You know the tried and true "let the eldest and the longest-tenured guy in the company teach the class" program. Or better yet, "let the top salesman teach the other salesman." Or even one better, the "send everyone to Tony Robbins training program!" Now, no offense, I happen to like Tony. This is referencing the types of programs companies produce that are a one-shot deal. They have a tremendous impact when they happen, but their effect wears off after the last donut is eaten. The Culture Cycle kicks in, and the Programming takes over.

We never caught on to the motivational speaker game until one day several years ago when I was at an event in Dallas with Zig Ziglar. Did you ever notice how many great stories motivational speakers tell about attendees sharing how much their life has changed since the first two times they saw them speak? Now, this may sound like a testimonial to the training they received, but if the training was so great, why do they keep coming back?

In defense of Ziglar and all the others, most people come in so pumped up that they will automatically leave feeling good. They were self-motivated. This is not America's workforce. What was the motivation of the Ziglar conference attendees? The $495 they spent to be there! Once the excitement has worn off and it's time to start doing the things Ziglar and Robbins and the Joel Olsteen types are suggesting, most people will not follow through. That's why they fail, and that's why they attend again and again and again.

Now, I must put myself in this boat as well because I have dozens of books written by these authors. And I used to find myself constantly referring to them for reinforcement. But the two morals of this story are:

1. You must have a system that is repetitive and provides for learning if you expect adults to grow.

2. Wouldn't it be great if people were as excited to come to your training class as they were Stephen Colbert's? Well, they can be. As a matter of fact, they must be!

Training is a topic very near and dear to my heart because this is where I see most companies fail with their attempts at culture change. The failure occurs mainly because their training and development philosophy is grounded in putting people through classes and calling them trained.

Now, combine that with the fact that today's generations demand development from their employers or they will move on which means they desire *real development* and not a certificate. Remember the list of things a Millennial or Gen Z worker wants from an employer? Number one was development. They want to grow professionally as well as personally. And they want their employer to provide that training.

So before we can move on, we must have some working definitions in place. These definitions are the basis for a lot of the information in this book and serve as the firm foundation of this specific topic.

Principle 1: What is learning?

How would you define learning? We have asked this question literally thousands of times to groups all across the country and typically get the same responses. Most people will define learning as "the process of acquiring knowledge." That is why we say that someone who has a degree from a university is a "learned" (pronounced learn ehd) person.

Question: How many degree-bearing individuals do you know who haven't got a clue? Right away, you are probably saying your boss or coworkers around you. (Before we go casting stones, remember the verse in the Bible about the log in your eye?) But these people do exist. It is possible to go through years of schooling and still not learn anything. I have a PhD, and my wife still wonders how I got it sometimes.

So when challenged with this fact, the groups then respond, "Well, it's not just acquiring the knowledge, but what you do with it." Exactly. Remember the adage Knowledge is Power? Well, throw that one away. **Knowledge itself is not power.** Having the knowledge does not automatically make one powerful. **It's what you do with the knowledge that determines how powerful you are.**

One of the key factors in creating an experience culture is to take the knowledge of the people in your organization and put it to use. In other words, you want them to do the things you are covering in the training class every day at work. This is the true way to capture the hearts and heads of the employees.

There are only three reasons why you won't get the results you desire from your training:

1.   **The teacher is not motivated.**
2.   **The students are not motivated.**
3.   **The topic is not motivated.**

Be careful not to confuse yourself here and read the word above as motivation*al*. There is a big difference. Motivational training is designed to make one feel good. It's a "pump you up" session that has short-term effect and results. When I say the training must be motivated, we are referring to the type of training. Let me explain.

In 1995, after spending several years in the field of training, I wanted to see if I really knew anything about training and development. So I signed up to attend Texas A&M University's Training and Development Certification Program. You see at the time, there was no such thing as a training and development degree, so this was as close as I could get. When completed, I could add the letters CTP after my name same as an accountant can add CPA after he gets his certification.

This particular program was designed in cooperation with the American Society of Training and Development. Throughout the course, each segment or module was taught by someone different – someone who by design was supposed to be the most knowledgeable person on the topic.

While some of the speakers were really good, there were several that were way off base. They had spent their entire career in school, and they had the PhDs to prove it. However, all this knowledge was theory and never put to practice by them. And, if we never put something to practice, we will not learn from it. School is based on reading or studying about other men's opinions and experiences. Life - especially in the business world - is about living it. These college professors were very intelligent and deserved my respect for their knowledge, but I'm not sure how much they "learned" from their schooling. A degree does not make one learned. (By the way, neither does writing a book!)

Question: How many people working for your company right now know what to do? How many of them are doing it? If you are like most owners or managers, then the answer to the second question is much smaller. If the answer is the same, why are you reading this book?

Learning then, by definition, is **a change in behavior**. We must see the behaviors of the individuals we are training change positively. That is the purpose of training. Written tests are wonderful to check retention and potential, but the true test is 90 days down the road when their behaviors are consistent with what you have trained – **not because you are watching, but because they have added a new skill to their daily routine.**

The three reasons listed above as to why training fails, it shows that if we are not facilitating training that is designed to produce **a change in behavior**, then the topic and the trainer are not motivated. But, all training is designed to change behavior. At least it should be. That's why we have it! Well, if that were true then…well, read on.

Principle 2: Teaching vs. Training

The most common method used to prepare people for their work assignments is teaching. Now I must tell you that if you are a school or academic teacher what you are about to read carries a Surgeon General's warning. I know you will read it anyway, but the next principle is not popular amongst the academia.

The purpose of teaching is to get the notes of the teacher transferred to the notes of the student. In other words, get my notes (teacher) to your notes (student.) When this has been accomplished, then teaching has done its job. This is a fairly straightforward definition but is accurate in its purest form.

We give the lectures. They take the notes. We give them a test. They pass it. We give them an 8.5" x 11" color glossy certificate to hang up on the wall. At the completion of this cycle, everyone has been taught, and we can expect all of the problems to go away and the performances to improve. Right?

The problem with the terms teaching and training are they are used interchangeably by people all the time. But they are two **VERY different** things. While teaching is defined as getting the information or knowledge from the teacher's notes to the students, the definition of training takes it one step further.

While training still has to complete the same steps as teaching to be successful, it adds three other "stops" along the way. More on those in just a minute.

Training is defined as getting the information from the teacher's notes to the student's notes, but it must touch the hearts and the heads of the individuals along the way. We have been talking this entire book about the importance of getting the hearts and the heads of the individuals involved in the workplace. Remember, one of the keys to culture change is that Everything Speaks! Every part of your business and its processes and systems must align with your philosophy of providing a Culturrific! Experience. Training is no different.

TEACHING IS PASSING ON KNOWLEDGE

TRAINING IS PASSING ON PERFORMANCE

With this simple explanation, we can see a huge difference. You are trying to develop an experience culture, and that requires performance. It requires your employees to deliver every customer every time. Training is only effective if it changes behavior. And it can only work if the trainer can perform what he or she is training.

Earlier we made the statement that most company's culture changes crash here because they don't understand the importance of training. Well, it's not so much that they don't understand the importance of training as much as it is they don't understand the "how" of training. In other words, the training is not motivated.

If you had a dollar for every time, you attended a speech that touted training as the number-one priority or said "training is of vital importance to our company; you would quite wealthy and would not need to read this book or any other non-fiction book. (Or would it be a fiction book in this context?) So, maybe you work for a company that places importance on training. If you do, then congratulations, because everything we have talked about in this book revolves around training and your success depends on it.

We must move beyond the traditional didactic approaches to teaching and start **training our people**. Think back to those professors at Texas A&M University. I knew some of them were off-base when they said that people (your trainees) don't need to know the "why," just give them the "how." (By the way, I sure enjoyed my time at A&M and hope that they don't get too angry with me about these comments and want my diploma back.)

Now, how many times have you been delegated an assignment without being given any input as to why you were chosen, why they needed it so quickly and whose bright idea it was anyway? We may all be workers, but we are trying to build an experienced team of thinkers as well as doers. We don't want people who act like robots and perform their functions. We want people who will **delight** the customer, not just satisfy them. There are too many people doing what you do, and society is too fickle to wait around for you to get your act together. Remember, **if you don't exceed their expectations, they will go somewhere else.**

Trainers focus on the "why" as well as the "how." They want to make sure the student understands the whole picture, not just their small part of it. Trainers also look for creative and innovative ways to involve the students that do not involve PowerPoint slides! Remember, when the lights go down in the room, they also go down in the minds of your student.

Training is the key, not just teaching. And learning - **a change in behavior** - is our goal. After all, your overall objective is to "program" new behavior into your culture. You have established what the values and beliefs are of your new culture, and through your learning about the culture cycle, we know that repetition is vital to programming your new experience culture.

There are three "stops" (mentioned earlier) on the road to making your training successful:

1. **Start with culture training and end with culture training.**
2. **Produce training that is consistent with your new culture.**
3 **Create a Learning University.**

Number three on the list above is so important that it rates its own chapter. We will deal with learning universities in the next chapter.

What do I mean by number one? You have spent the first five stops on your journey designing your new experience culture. You have established that for it to work, you need to capture the **hearts and heads of your employees**, not just their hands and feet. There is about to be sweeping changes in the everyday life of every employee at your company. The first task your training and development department should be assigned to create a series of culture training classes for everyone (and we do mean everyone) to attend.

These regular seminars are designed to communicate the new culture to your employees. It is not enough to produce a fancy graphic or document detailing your new beliefs, values, and accepted behaviors; you must develop training classes to help your employees understand each of these new items. What do you mean by integrity? What does Disney mean when they say Quality Guest Experience?

This is where your culture starts to take shape quickly. But your "bus" will come to a screeching halt into the embankment if you do not follow item number two above – produce training that is consistent with your new culture.

Here I'm referring to the elimination of the old methods and lecture styles and put in new experience-oriented training methods. You need to make a significant impact on your employees that sends the message, "Things are going to be different around here from now on." How can you possibly do this with a lecture? Or, worse yet, many companies will want to skip items one and two here altogether and handle it over a conference call!

Acting out Your New Experience Culture

One of the best practices we have found when trying to train a person about your culture is through acting. The more familiar term for this is **role-playing**, but I think there is a difference between the two. Role-playing tends to engage only one side of the scenario. For example, if you are role-playing a sales presentation, the person who is being trained is the salesman, not the customer. But there is so much valuable information and knowledge that could be put to use when you are playing the part of the customer – **especially if you are trying to grow an experience culture.**

In acting, you are engaging all parties in the training. You are just as concerned with the knowledge the salesperson is getting as you are the knowledge the person playing the customer is getting. You can even have them dress up in costumes to add to the effect. To reach their hearts, they have to feel it. In role-playing, you do not involve the whole person, just the hands, and feet.

The truth is the most powerful and effective tool in the training and development of your team is role-play. Whether you're working on selling skills, service skills or product knowledge, role-play can be an effective tool in changing a salesperson's behavior.

Acting (Role-play) As a Training Tool

Acting or role-play is probably the least favorite training tool for employees. But here's the truth: Everyone role-plays. You either role-play with a manager in a learning environment where you can grow and develop practicing the "right way," or you can role-play with the customer. ***The difference is that one of these methods costs you money and one makes you money.***

Acting in a controlled environment allows you to check for understanding with your tram. They'll always say yes if you ask them if they "got it" after training. Acting lets you see for yourself if they truly did get it. The principle of primacy, one of the principles of learning, says that people remember what they heard first. This means that if they see and learn the right way first, that's what they'll remember. If they see and learn the wrong way first, they'll remember that. So if they're allowed to "practice" new skills on a customer versus in the training class, the chances that they'll do it incorrectly are very high. And since that's what they'll remember, so all your hard work and effort goes to waste.

It's important to set the stage for the employee when you're using acting. Let him know that it's a safe environment. Communicate why you're asking him or her to do this. No one likes change, and you're effectively asking him to change so you can anticipate some apprehension and pushback.

Acting is a pressure-cooker environment. You'll hear your people say "But I'm so much better with customers." **Of course, they are — the customer doesn't know they're doing it wrong!** Put the person at ease and assure her that the purpose of acting isn't to catch her doing something wrong but to teach her to do it right. Encourage her by sharing your thoughts on acting and role-play, such as how you get nervous when asked to role-play in front of your peers, too. When possible, do the acting technique with just you and the employee, not in front of the whole team. Millennials tend to be more at ease in front of the group, but your veterans probably won't be.

I role-play in front of the whole group when I do training seminars, but the people don't know each other. I use the group to provide feedback and use each role-play to benefit everyone in the room. But you can follow a simpler process.

Tips to Master the Art of Acting

Here are 5 Tips to master the art of acting in your training:

1   **Start small**. Don't try to address an entire process or procedure or sales presentation at once. Focus on one part of the process. This allows you to drill down and focus on a specific skill. If you try and do too much, you'll overwhelm the learner, and your effectiveness starts to go down. For example, role-play just the greeting with a customer and not the whole sales or service process. The other benefit of keeping things "small" is that it's less intimidating for the employee. He doesn't have as much to remember, and there are fewer chances for it to go wrong

2   **Be specific**. Give feedback on their performance after the role-play, and be specific. Avoid blanket phrases like, "You did a really good job." Instead, tell him exactly what you liked or didn't like. You might say, "I really liked how you used my name." This gives clear direction to the learner and ensures that your feedback is heard and received. It also dramatically increases the learning since affirmation calls attention to a specific skill.

3 **Be real**. Too many managers think their role is to try and "trip up" the employee. In fact, this detracts from learning. Be real. Act like a real customer. **Act out scenarios that represent the majority, not the minority** — be the customer that most typically comes into your store or works with your company, not the one who engages you once every so often. For example, if your salespeople are ready for the majority, your sales will go up much faster than if you focus on the minority. And if your phone support team is focused on the typical customer conversation, then the experience for all the customers will improve.

4 **Be equal**. This one might sound funny, but the principle is simple: Treat every employee in your company equally. This doesn't mean you have to treat them the same. If you have a veteran person who is a top performer, you will handle this person's role-play differently than a rookie that just started two months ago. The key is that *both* need you to role-play with them. Don't make the mistake of believing that acting is only for the rookie.

5 **Debrief**. It is the "debrief" of the acting that is most critical. You are not looking for what was done right and what was done wrong. You are looking for how it felt to be in this scenario – from both sides! This is where the difference between role-playing and acting really comes to light.

Try asking questions like:

- How did you feel when Brayden asked you to buy a higher-priced model?
- How did you feel when Madeline said no to you?
- How did you feel having to tell Ray that his reservation had been cancelled and there were no more rooms?
- How did it feel to be traveling all day and have your reservation gone?
- How did you feel when Christine found you a room at another location and arranged to have milk and cookies waiting for you in the competitor's hotel to say sorry?

Starting to get it? These questions tap into the very heart of the scenarios you are using to train your employees. They must **feel** to be empathetic. We have also found that by dressing them up, they take on a true character and add more realism to the part. People are not afraid to act since they are not being themselves (even though they are).

6　**Use video**. Record the acting when possible. This allows the employee to see exactly what you're referring too as you give feedback. But make sure you delete the video when you're done and promise them it will not end up on Twitter, Instagram or social media. The video is for you and the employee only — no one else.

The most important aspect of acting is that you follow up. Watch your employees in action and listen to find out if they're using the new skills or simply selling the old way. The true test is when the employee thinks no one is watching. If he's using the new skills, make sure you praise and encourage him. **What gets rewarded gets repeated**.

Having a culture of acting in your company is a tremendous advantage over your competition. Employees feel a strong sense of accountability to the training and new skills because they know you're watching them, both during the training and after. In my 30 years of training and development of salespeople, I've never found or used a more effective tool than this. The immediate repetition and practice coupled with the accountability of performing the skill is the best way to **change behavior**. It gives you the chance to praise and encourage the employee, which is always a plus for performance.

Another part of being consistent with your culture is who attends these classes. **EVERYONE!** The CEO, the VPs, no one is to miss these classes – PERIOD! Also, do not divide or segregate the classes by department or hierarchy. The VP must be mixed in with the part-timer. The front line needs to see that what is happening is real and believed by the top. Every great leadership book will tell you that it starts at the top. If you have an executive who feels his time is too valuable to be messing with such trivial things as culture classes and acting, then you probably have an opening for a new executive.

Herb Kelleher, the former CEO of Southwest Airlines, is best known for his time spent each month either taking tickets at the gate or loading luggage on the ramp. (Everything Speaks) **There are no small parts, just small actors**. This means that no one person is any more important than any other. This is VITAL in an experience culture. Everyone needs to feel that his or her role is important and appreciated.

The Culture Class (Ongoing)

Earlier, I gave you the instructions to create a series of culture seminars for your existing employees to start weaving together the fabric of your new Culturrific! Experience culture. But, there are two culture classes, which need to be developed.

The "series" for the existing employees and the culture class that would resemble Disney's "Traditions" class. This culture class is your new employee's first day. They are not to be allowed to report to their department until they have met this requirement. Thought I would throw that in one more time with repetition being the mother of learning, and because I am not the only one who feels this way.

Hal Rosenbluth in his book, The Customer Comes Second, describes the orientation process of a new employee at Rosenbluth travel agency. As the CEO, Hal believed his most important role was to carry on the traditions started by his great-grandfather in the business when it was founded in 1892. (That's a lot of folklore!) One of the greatest tasks for Hal was the preservation of the culture of Rosenbluth. They attribute their success to the power of their culture and the culture training they did for every employee. Hal eventually sold the agency to American Express for a reported $350M. In a statement about the acquisition, American Express listed the Rosenbluth culture as a key reason they wanted to buy the company.

You may have a company that hires only a few people at a time. Perhaps you only cast one or two people a week or a month. And it could be a real challenge to try acting and teambuilding with one person. In this case, create a "Culture Lite" class for the new employee. This would be a shortened one-on-one class given to the new employee by your trainer. At the end of the month, hold a complete culture class and have everyone hired during that month attend. This would also apply to companies with multiple locations such as a retailer or restaurant who trains in the field at each location.

What goes in the culture class? Here is a list of the best stuff to include:

- Definition of culture
- Your Company Folklore
- Your Product
- Your Vision (deal with each value and guiding principle)
- Your Purpose
- Your Experience Formula
- Your HR stuff (rules, benefits, dress code, etc.)
- Your Expectations of them in their Role
- Your Vocabulary (if necessary)
- Your Training and Development Plans for Them

Again, when preparing this class, use different techniques to send your culture message. Two things we have always used in the past that have worked well are mental aerobics and physical aerobics. We recommend these techniques for all your training, not just your culture class.

We start each training class with a physical aerobics activity. No, this is not a Pilate's class, but activities designed to get the class up and get their blood pumping. You know how dead the room is when you start a class so put some excitement in it. These activities also send the message of "team" each time you do them since they are team-based, not individual-based.

We do things from our Vacation Bible School days like relay races, drawing races, and other competitive aerobics. These are not icebreakers. The point of physical aerobics is that the student's mind is anywhere but in the classroom when they arrive. They are thinking about last night, the ball game on Sunday, the report they have due that they would much rather be working on right now, and so on. This aerobics clear the mind and get the student focused in the room. It's part of our "BE HERE NOW" principle of training.

After they complete the physical aerobics, then it's time for Mental Aerobics. Yes, it's that time when we find out who studied and who didn't since the last class. You are going for a review of the information covered so far and laying the springboard for today's training topic. These mental aerobic activities (more commonly known as quizzes or tests) send the message that you are serious about learning in your organization. **They also provide for another repetition of the training materials and "program" the culture cycle one more time.**

Some rules about mental aerobics (quizzes):

1. Always make them multiple choice. Precise recall or fill in the blanks are not good measures of knowledge. They are good measures of memorization. Remember, knowledge is not power; it's potential.
2. Always give at least four responses to each question for them to choose from.
3. Use this rule for your answers – give one that is exactly right, one that is totally wrong and two that, if they did not study, could be argued they are correct responses. As a matter of fact, at the top of each of our mental aerobics, put the disclaimer "Read every question carefully as there may be more than one right answer. Select the answer that is *most often* correct." Now that's measuring learning.
4. Review the answers in class together. As you read over each question, use it as a discussion period to run through the material again. The purpose of a test is to check retention. The purpose of mental aerobics is also to check for retention, but it adds repetition as well.

We usually spend the first hour of every day of our training programs completing these two aerobic exercises. It prepares the student for our form of learning – **a change in behavior!**

Once your training and development team has created the first series of culture classes and created the new employee orientation culture class, then they are ready to move onto their next task—creating a learning university. It's the next level of people development that will show your next generation employees that you are serious about their training and development.

But it's important to start with the principles of training in this chapter. Too many companies jump right to the "structure" and topics of classes and toss learning to the side. They assume exposure to the topic is the same thing as learning it. But you know that is wrong (and a bit sad.)

Reflections

What are the most important takeaways you got from this chapter?

What are some of the challenges you see when trying to get these ideas implemented?

Who else in your organization needs to read and understand this?

Establishing a Learning University

No train. No Gain.

That subtitle quote sums it all up so well. No training of our employees means no gaining in our sales or service or bottom line profits. Corporate Universities are one the buzzwords of the HR world. But for many companies, creating a corporate university is a fad or trend. Read this chapter very carefully to understand what a corporate university was designed to be and why I use the term learning university instead.

In analyzing what's going on out there, I have discovered that there are four types or forms of corporate universities in place today. They are the Moniker University, the Salaried University, the Building University and the Learning University. These types really could be defined as stages as most companies seem to pass through all of them on their journey to the perfect corporate university. Let's define each type.

Type I - The Moniker University

This is the most common type in use today. It is also the easiest one to create. Our friends at the American Heritage Dictionary define moniker as "nickname" and, basically, that is all this type of corporate university is. The Moniker University requires some creative artwork and new letterhead. The training and development department of your company creates a new logo and pronounces themselves at a ribbon cutting ceremony as a corporate university. They probably even have some clever name for it like Teach U. The error and ineffectiveness in this first type is that no fundamental changes in the way of doing business or in their methods or approaches to training are made. The company is simply trending on the bandwagon trying not to be outdone. It's truly just a rebranding of HR in some aspects. These types of universities hurt the furthering of the corporate university concept. If you are currently a Moniker, stop it!

Type II - The Salaried University

This type of university completes step one from above by pronouncing itself a university and creating a new logo with sweatshirts and the like. The company may even take it one step further and change some of its ways of doing things to incorporate a few traditional university methods. This type is even on record for producing a catalogue or phrasing all courses as "101s." The difference between the Salaried University and the others is where they focus their time. The Salaried University, as its name leads you to surmise, focuses on management or the salaried individuals running the company. They tend to ignore the hourly people, except of course for the 1.5-hour orientation slide show; everyone is required to attend, including black and white photos of the founder and the first whatever you made.

A presentation like this certainly says, "You have come to some place special." (By the way, that is sarcasm.) Orientations like this one described violate one of the three reasons training is not successful – **this training is not motivated!**

How can you build an experience culture if the only people your training services is the top line? **The front line is where your identity as a top experience provider is created**. The hourly people, not the salaried people, are the ones who will determine if you have an experience culture. A side note to companies with this type of university is they tend to have the highest turnover for two reasons:

1. The front line people get frustrated and tired of feeling stupid (unappreciated) because they are not being trained or developed.
2. The salaried people get great training and then move onto the next job. They get tired of hearing the hourly people complain about how bad it is!
3. Millennials and Gen Z people will not tolerate it. They will leave.

Question. How much time does your management spend servicing the customer? Another question. How much time does the hourly staff spend servicing your customer? Then why would you invest your training dollars at the salaried level? Oh, because you are training your managers to train their people? Yea, that is a dream world, and we all know it.

Type III - The Building University

The most expensive of all of the corporate universities, the Building University, picks up where the Salaried left off and provides a beautiful state-of-the-art structure to fly people in from all over the country or even from around the world to attend school. I attended a presentation at a conference where two companies, the Bank of Montreal and Motorola, were proudly displaying the pictures of their corporate universities.

Although Motorola does one of the better jobs with the corporate university concept, how many of us have companies that can afford to build $30,000,000 buildings? Can you imagine? How much training could you do on the front lines where it is needed with $30 million? The last thing you want to do is invest your money in glitzy, state-of-the-art buildings. You want to put your money into making sure the training is motivated. A glamorous trip to headquarters for training is impressive, but if the student leaves without a change in behavior, then it doesn't matter what cool stuff they did while they were there.

McDonald's Hamburger University (one of the country's first) is a classic example of this type. They also qualify for the Type II as well, because the only people who are allowed to attend the training are the managers. I also use McDonalds here to illustrate that while I am down on these first three types of corporate university structures, they can still have some effect. A Big Mac in Indiana tastes the same as the one in Texas and as the one in Manilla (I've tested this theory many times around the world.) So, they are having some level of success. It's simply that I believe there is another level – a level that we need to explore to produce an "experience" and not just a tasty burger.

Type IV - The Learning University

Okay, maybe calling the fourth type the Learning University is a little self–serving, but if you are set on the journey to culture change and building a Culturrific! Experience in your company, then you need this fourth type. And, if you build any other it will not be as successful. Yes, if you build it they will come, but don't forget the definition of learning – **a change in behavior**. If you can accomplish this change without building large structures of steel and concrete are you not better served?

The majority of you reading this book work for companies that have multiple locations or regions. You need to build a training process that will work in this environment. The Type IV University does this. But it doesn't just dress itself up like a traditional university.

The successful corporate university models itself after a traditional university - the *whole* university. How so? Well, there are five things that all traditional universities have that make them successful. And these five things must be present in your corporate university as well.

And the five are:

1. **Degree Plans**
2. **Course Numbering**
3. **Structure**
4. **Marketing**
5. **Campus Life**

Degree Plans

All traditional universities group their courses or curriculum into degree plans. These degree plans help the student and the teacher to know what subjects they must complete to be able to go into the real world and say they are ready. As we noted earlier, just because a person has a degree from a university does not mean you are learned. The degree simply means the person has the potential to excel and do well when put in an environment that allows him to use this teaching.

The people of the business-training world will call these topics **core competencies**. What does that mean? Well, like all great associations and organizations, the ability to create new and wieldy terms with words from Jeopardy is their reason for existence. In a nutshell, though, core competencies are the skills that one needs to do his or her job effectively and efficiently. As a matter of fact, our friends at the American Heritage Dictionary define competency as "a specific range of skill, knowledge or ability." The core competencies are the specific skills, knowledge or abilities broken down by position.

What the professional trainers (or your HR directors) are saying makes sense and it fits in with the experience culture theme. To be effective, the employees need to have the skills, knowledge, and ability for their specific job assignments. For you to create degree plans for your company, you must first decide what core competencies are needed for each position – that's right – EVERY position. By now, you should have picked up on a strong theme in this book that says, "There are no small parts, only small actors." I hope you are noticing this.

But how do you know what the core competencies should be for the degree plans? You ask the people who work for you. After all, they are the ones who know best what it takes to do their jobs well. If you're lucky, many may have already been accomplished by the HR or Training teams. Great! Use them.

The research for defining core competencies this has four steps:

1. the written
2. the interview
3. the analysis
4. the competencies

The Written

Step one in this process is to have the two top performers in each department (or role) create a list of what they do each day. Have them be very specific. Give each of the respondents a written form to complete. Be careful not to be too leading on this form. Do not have them answer questions like "Do you think good grammar is important in your job?" If this question is burning in your heart and keeps you up at night, save it for step two of the process. The answers you get to these types of questions are no help. It is advisable, though, to give them some leading examples of what you are looking for to get them started. Then have them complete the training they think someone needs to be able to perform these job functions on their list.

Next, have the newest person in each department (or role) complete the same exercise. This will show what should have been covered in the initial training for new employees. Also, this is a fresh mind that has not been diluted with thoughts of "that's just the way we do things around here." The new employees will also be much more forthcoming and honest with you. After all, they don't know any better yet. Finally, have two medium-to-low producers in each department complete the exercise.

By now, you have probably seen the wisdom of gathering the information from all levels in each role or department. It will be very interesting to compare the lists from each group. You may find some very intriguing holes. Hopefully, you find some consistent themes, though.

Now, have the manager of each department complete the same task and add his or her list to the groups. The further up you go with this research, the more interesting. It has been shown in many companies that the further from the front line a person is, the less they know about what is needed to do that job successfully. And of course, whoa to those companies who have managers, directors, and VPs who spend three hours every other month on the front lines or answering telephones only to come back to the next big meeting and say, "Boys, this is what's going on down there!"

When step one is completed, you will have information from the following in each department:

1	Manager and/or director
2	Top performers
2	Medium to low performers
1	Newest person

The Interview

Step two of the process is to schedule an interview with each of the respondents on your research. Many times the answers given can be interpreted wrong or what the respondent meant was not what they wrote. It's very hard to transfer to paper what one thinks. A verbal response can be very powerful. But do NOT try to shortcut this process and only do the verbal part. Make sure they bring their written assignment with them. If they show up to the interview without it, send them home. Their information will be from the hip and certainly not what you want to use to leverage your company's investment.

You must be very careful during this part of the process not to lead them in any way. You may ask them some questions to check assumptions or find out if they agree with others, but make sure all of this information is confidential. You are not part of a Mission Impossible episode, but if people know their answers will not be broadcast or come back to haunt them, they will be more forthcoming. Also, we have found in these sessions that employees may try to turn it into a gripe session about their boss or job. Keep them on track.

What you are looking for are the key skills, knowledge, and abilities for someone in each of your departments. When you have compiled the lists successfully, you will have your "core competencies." But more importantly, you will have the basis for your degree plans.

The Analysis

Step three of the process is to narrow down the lists by taking items listed only once by one person or items that make no sense and throw them out. You cannot possibly use every suggestion and must cull your lists down. Imagine how overwhelming it would be to give a new employee a list of 47 things they must learn to be able to do their job!

This is the easiest step of the process. It can be done in one day. During the analysis, you will find it necessary to consult with the interviewees to check for accuracy and understanding. You might even consider doing further interviews with other parties to check for validity of your findings.

The Competencies

Step four of the process is to categorize the topics under subject headers. For example, one department might comment on telephone skills, another on telephone selling, a third on using the telephone and finally one on learning how to transfer a call without sending the person to phone hell. All of these topics can be grouped together under Telephone Skills.

This fourth step incorporates more than one principle from above – the degree plan and also the course numbering system. We will talk more about course numbering in just a few pages because you may not want to take it to that level at this time. You can still have the same success with your university by using the title of the class without giving it a number.

The purpose of grouping the subjects under titles is to see if you have classes that could be developed to encompass more than one topic. The rule is very simple here – Is what the people are suggesting a true training need or just an execution problem? For example, let's stay with phones for a minute. Let's say that management has determined that we need to answer the phones on the third ring and in their infinite wisdom has prescribed a training class to make this happen.

First, exactly how long of a class do you need to train someone they should answer the phone on the third ring? About long enough to bring everyone in the room, let the phone ring three times, pick it up, answer it and ask if there are any questions. Of course, you could go further and give a more dramatic presentation, but Best Training Course on Answering the Phone on the Third Ring will never be a category in the Training and Development Emmys. So, why waste your time?

Don't Meet, Train.

One of the main reasons it is hard to get people to come to your training classes is because many of them can be handled in a simple meeting or memo. Remember point two in the last chapter about the success of your training – the students must be motivated. **This is exactly why many employees come to your training very unmotivated.**

What is the difference between a meeting and a training session? It goes right back to the difference between teaching and training – a change in behavior is our goal, AND we are trying to touch the hearts and heads of every employee in the process. No one likes meetings. The very sound of the word conjures up visions of glazed eyes and glazed donuts…neither of which are any good.

It will be very important for you to only produce training classes that are worthy of your university curriculum degree plans and are also motivated. Use this as your litmus test. Never let any training class go on that is not worth at least one hour of the employee's time. The recommended length would be two hours. That may scare a lot of your budgets, but it is necessary if you wish to create an experience culture. Remember, if the class is boring, not useful or not worthy of the employee's time, the next time you have a class the attendance will be nil. This happens a lot when you try to do a training class on a topic that is not training, but rather a disciplinary or execution problem. Consider this –

The training class is itself an experience so make sure it is one that would be worthy of the experience you want them to provide your customers.

You will need to create a degree plan for every position listing the core competencies for each position. Make sure you are looking at the person as a whole. So far, we are only looking at the process side of your culture; but you will need to add the people side to your degree plans as well.

Keep Them Hired

Now for the real beauty of degree plans – employee retention and morale. I have written consistently in this book that the front line is the bottom line. Your guiding principle should be— **treat your people with an experience the way you want your people to treat your customer with an experience.** Show your people they are valued, and they will value what your company stands for.

Imagine this. You are sitting with an employee going through her annual review. She has been with you for one year now, and you are discussing her future with your company when suddenly you pop the big question, "Where do you see yourself going in this company in the next year?" We have all asked this question. Some of you even have forms that must be completed on this very topic. I'm not big on forms like this, but degree planning has become our answer to this uncomfortable situation.

It is very hard for a manager and an employee to sit and discuss the employee's strengths and weaknesses. It is uncomfortable and stressful on both parties, which is why the review forms HR gets back are so poorly completed. Degree plans accomplish the same objective, but in an environment that is comfortable for both parties. Therefore, the exchange is much freer and more realistic.

In the degree plan scenario, when the employee says "I see myself becoming the supervisor this year," you say "Well, let's look at what degree you need to get there." Simple. It is just like when you were in high school or college. Someone sat down with you and asked, "What do you want to be when you grow up?" The person proceeds to select a degree for you that would prepare you for this new life. The degree was broken into a plan of specific courses and requirements you had to meet to be qualified to earn the degree. The same is true for your corporate university.

Once you have defined what position they want, you then create a degree plan for them to get there. The courses required have already been determined in the steps above. You are simply highlighting them and creating a schedule to complete the courses based on the offering and the employee's time. Now that's exciting! And that's a way to make someone feel like he or she is special and an important part of your culture. It also supports the notion that there must be constant training in the employee's career with you. Remember, if you do not develop your employees, they will go somewhere else and find someone who will. It would be terrible to lose the great talent your "casting directors" found for you.

Also, this information you have now uncovered is the basis for the Performer Profiles discussed in the "Casting" chapter, page 211.

What's in a Degree Plan?

A quality degree plan seeks to develop the entire employee – their work skills, their intellectual skills, and their personal skills. There must be a balance between personal and professional in the degree plan. This is vital when you think about the self-esteem employees are drawing from their jobs. If you do not develop them, they will lose confidence in themselves and stop thinking freely, which means you have lost their heads and their hearts will soon follow.

Each degree plan should have courses from the following four areas:

Degree

Operational
Role Specific
Personal
Customer Relations
Culture

In the Purpose chapter and the next chapter, we support the fact that for your culture's values to have any hope of becoming your employee's values, you need to tie compensation and promotion to them. The degree plan is designed to help you do this.

When an employee completes a degree, then qualify them for an increase in their rate of pay. You know that the training equips them to do a better job for you, so reward them for completing it. Of course, you should not hand them a raise without checking for competency first. That is where your mental aerobics and your follow up come in.

In one of my past lives, we created two degrees that an employee could earn – the bachelors and the masters. (Sounds very original doesn't it.) There were three requirements to complete the degree and get the pay raise.

1. They had to pass a written test.
2. They had to complete a course on their responsibilities once they received the degree. The beauty of our program was that not only did they get a raise; they got a promotion with added responsibilities.
3. They had to pass a formal review process by their manager and the other employees who already held the degree. (A sort of degree-granting committee.)

This proved to be a strong motivator for the employees. Imagine the hourly people asking to go to training. And since we followed the principles outlined in this book, we knew the more training we gave them, the more "programming" we were doing of our experience culture.

An employee should be allowed to pursue multiple degrees, but only one degree at a time. Below is an excerpt from one of the catalogues that my team developed and we used successfully. It shows a more advanced system but gives you an idea as a starting point.

Bachelor Degree Plans

<u>College of Catering</u>   8 Core, 8 General Studies

Core:

3	1000-1099	Scene Operations
3	1100-1199	Scene Policies and Procedures
2	1200-1299	Conference Center Principles
0	1300-1399	Critical Success Selling

General Studies:

3	1400-1499	Guest Relations
2	1500-1599	Loss Prevention/Safety
0	1600-1699	Specialty
3	1700-1799	Personal Development

In this scenario, you will see that the degree plan has been broken into two types of credits received by the employees when they complete the course. They are Core and General Studies. The Core credits were set aside for the operational or process half of the culture. These were the ones that focused on the core competencies drawn from the Performer Profiles. The General Studies courses were more for the people side of the culture.

In this learning university, employees needed 16 total credits to be eligible for their raise and degree, and the credits needed were specific to their job. This was for a hotel/conference canter. In this case, the roles of each person varied greatly, but there were many similarities between positions. Therefore, we took another page from the traditional university and broke the degree plans into colleges all under the single university.

These colleges each had a Dean who was the head of that area. In this example, the College of Catering included all of the Food and Beverage functions of the hotel, including restaurants, break services, private dining, and off-site catering. The employees would be separated under different supervisors and may not see each other on any given day since they were so spread out in the building. But their training needs were the same.

Here is another page from that same catalogue, which shows a different college. Notice how the degree plan still has the same structure, but what credits are needed has changed based on the roles of the people this college serves.

A degree plan must always have the same amount of credits in each college, or you will be in for serious trouble, especially if you tie it to pay raises.

<u>College of Service</u>   8 Core, 8 General Studies

Core:

3	1000-1099	Scene Operations
2	1100-1199	Scene Policies and Procedures
2	1200-1299	Conference Center Principles
1	1300-1399	Critical Success Selling

General Studies:

4	1400-1499	Guest Relations
2	1500-1599	Loss Prevention/Safety
0	1600-1699	Specialty
2	1700-1799	Personal Development

Course Numbering

Once you have decided on the core competencies by position and have listed them in degree plans, you are ready for the next step – course numbering. Earlier we said that you might not want to try this part. While it is true that you can have an effective and motivated training plan without numbering every course, let's take a look at the reasons "pro" numbering.

Tops on the list will be tracking. The title of a course or its objectives may change with time. As a matter of fact, they should. As new ideas and services are introduced, the curriculum should be updated. But the numbers can help track the progress.

If you are reading this book, you are most likely in a service or even retail or hospitality company. What is the one thing that drives your business? REPORTS! Lots and lots of number crunching analytical reports. Now, what is the biggest problem facing the training world? Proving its existence and effectiveness! With a course numbering system, you can create a database to give instant feedback on who is doing what. Your database can even create some exciting reports for the big guys! (They love this kind of thing.)

When I was working at one retail organization, we started with a Type I corporate university. We used course numbering simply to add effect. Everything was a 101 or 201 if it was more advanced. As we grew, we found that this actually did more harm than good. The numbers just added confusion; after all, they were of no value. They were just window dressing. A couple of years into it, we decided to model a true university and created a course numbering system similar to a university. We were short-sighted since we used three-digit course numbers. We quickly filled all of the available slots with courses and had nowhere to go.

When using course numbers, at the minimum, start at four digits. Do not get too carried away with this and have course numbers that look like the Dewey decimal system. This, again, will detract from the learning experience.

In our best days, we created a database and put a version at each of our 17 retail locations around the country. These locations were tracking all the activity each month and using the database to generate a monthly activity recap and sending to corporate for compilation. Imagine this; we knew exactly what training EACH person in the company had EACH month. Now that's exciting! None of this could be accomplished without the course numbering. (Incidentally, the database was revised to include all of the employee's personnel information as well. This gave us the ability to send birthday cards, and for our HR directors to track reviews and salary history. Of course, it was protected!)

The Type IV University was one that put the training on the front lines where it belonged. This practice is not new. It's been tried before. But it has always failed because there was no accountability. But with course numbering there is.

One last thought on why course numbering before we discuss how to do it. If you use the database or just do it on paper, tracking each employee's training progress will give a clear snapshot of who is ready for promotion. If you have an opening and three people apply (any of whom you think could fill it,) wouldn't it be great to be able to print out what training each one had completed to see who is most prepared? Well, it was when we did it.

The sample pages from the corporate university catalogue shown above give you an idea of what the course numbering is all about. Each level depicts a discipline that must be learned by the employee. What is not shown is how we take a level and break it down further like in the sample page below. Again, this is from the same book.

General Studies Course Numbers

1400	GUEST RELATIONS	Example of Class
1400-1409	Complaints	Handle a Complaint
1410-1419	The Life of a Guest	Guest Alienation
1420-1429	Difficult Guests	The Problem is…
1430-1439	Quality Guest Experience	Making it Inspirational
1440-1449	Empowerment	Handling it Alone
1450-1459	Dealing with Disabilities	Sign Language
1460-1469	Everything Speaks	Everything Speaks
1470-1479	Magical Rescues	Service Recovery
1480-1489	Independent Study	
1490-1499	Outside Teacher	

Notice how the course numbers have been further defined in this example by the degree plans shown above. Earlier we spoke of the power of knowing exactly what the people in the field are being trained on and here is the proof. In most companies (and in Type I-III universities), the most they could ever hope to know is that their people had customer service or in this example guest relations training.

What was the topic? Who knows? But with the system above, you can see that when one of your locations reports they held a 1450 course, they were covering how to deal with a guest with a disability. Now that's power. We are not going further in this book, but yes, you guessed it right, the levels are broken down even further. The more specific we can be, the greater our budget was each year when it came time to ask for money!

You may not do this portion of your university yet, but we hope you see the power in creating this level of commitment. This is only part of the structure you need to build an experience culture.

Structure

This is where we seem to run into the most roadblocks when working with companies in trying to help them set up their corporate university. Most find the degree plans and course numbering a great asset, even fun to do, but the structure part is hard. Why? Because it requires the buy-in and commitment from all levels within the company and we all know how hard that is. This one will be your toughest sell of the five, but it is also the one that will produce dramatic results. **The biggest problem we hear from companies is their attendance. Getting everyone to come to class is so hard for them. If this is the case, herein lies your answer.**

When we look at traditional universities, we see that one of their strengths is they have a structure for their classes. Part of that structure is the degree plan and course numbering, but the most important part is the predictability of the course offerings.

Traditional universities create a set schedule for their courses, which does not change. It is predictable and reduces confusion. If you are in Chemistry 2310, it meets in Room 310 every Monday, Wednesday, and Friday from 11:00 to 11:50 a.m. This class happens at the same time and in the same place every week. This means that the student doesn't have to worry about the semantics of the class, just the learning. And it eliminates the basis for many of the excuses people have for not showing up to class like, "I didn't know what room it was in."

Imagine the power of predictability in training in your company. If you are like 98% of the companies out there, you have training sporadically, and the attendance is poor at best. What if your department had training the same time, the same place every week? What would this do for you?

1. **Increase attendance**. Everyone can plan for it. It always amazes us how employees never forget their scheduled work times (which change weekly), but can't seem to remember their scheduled training time. This is an excuse. Eliminate it. Your experience culture is based on accountability. If someone does not attend a training class, he or she should be reprimanded the same as if they did not show up for a shift. It MUST carry the same weight if you expect to have any success building this new culture.
2. **Provide for scheduling ease**. One of the nightmares in a service company is scheduling. You have many hours to cover and lots of part-timers working for you. First, part-timers are just as important and should receive the same training. Second, if the manager has a set time for training each week, he or she can build a schedule far in advance.

The best practice of this principle I have seen is when a company took it one step further and had all departments hold their training at the same time. They chose Saturday and Sunday mornings with half the group coming in on Saturday and the other half coming in on Sunday. This was a seven-day-a-week operation, so the Sunday time was not a problem for them. This may not be the case for you, but the practice is sound.

Everyone in the building knew when the training was. The topics changed each week, and several classes were being held around the building at the same time to accommodate multiple degree plans. This company told us there was never a scheduling problem and the attendance had never been better. Plus, they received a boost in the morale of the company because they were getting together once a week like a family – an added bonus to building their service culture.

Marketing

Every great university (and even the not-so-great universities) in America today spends a nice percentage of its annual budget on marketing the university. You would think people would be thrilled to get an education anywhere and would simply go to the closest school, but this is certainly not the case. Is it because the education varies greatly from school to school? Somewhat. A serious student will want the best program. But in today's marketplace, it is very common to find people working in a position that has nothing to do with their degree. So the emphasis on "where" they get their degree is more a matter of marketing than it is true "education." (Yes, I know you got into tons of student loan debt because you went to the best school for your degree, but you are not the majority.)

What we do know is that there are some basic excepted perceptions by the American public (and **remember, perception is a reality even if it's not the truth**).

1. State university degrees carry more weight than community college degrees.
2. Ivy League degrees carry more weight than all of them.
3. Sports play a significant role in selecting a university.
4. The more you spend, the better the education.

We especially love the last one. It is the most widely believed of them all. But there is a common thread among all people who choose a university – the marketing of that university influences them. Even the cost of the tuition is a form of marketing.

Marketing takes on many different forms from posters, to television commercials, to admissions counselors who take the marketing message on the road. One thing is true; all universities are in competition just like your business. And the one that does the best job of marketing or selling itself wins the most times.

The theme of this chapter is that if you are going to be a learning university, then you need to act like a traditional university. What are some of the marketing ideas universities use that your learning university should model?

1.   Catalogue. All universities have a catalogue that explains the courses, who they are for, etc. But the catalogue also includes information on the degree plans and the other aspects of the university including campus life, which we will discuss next.
2.   Marketing Campaigns. Each year, the university tries to come up with some marketing slogan or campaign designed to increase enrollment and attendance. They even have marketing campaigns to keep up attendance. You would think that if someone were paying $80,000 for an education, they would go to class. But you also think that if the training was "required" in a company that everyone would go to the class as well! Neither of these is true.

The purpose of your marketing campaign is to get people motivated and excited about the training your company provides. In the three reasons training fails, one is because the student is not motivated. Here is where you attack this problem. In my retail days, we always took part of our budget for a new training program and used it on marketing. My favorite was the campaign for a new selling program we introduced. We had a selling process, which had served us well up to this point, but we were experimenting with incentive-based pay in some of our markets which were a shift from the non-commissioned environment we had been operating in since the beginning.

Our current process had four phases W-I-S-E (Welcome, Interview, Solution, and Experience). We had been teaching our employees that their role was to help the customer make an intelligent buying decision. It all played out very nicely. But we were now introducing a new program that not only modified our earlier philosophy but also had tremendous implications on our culture if it was not handled correctly.

We decided on a campaign using the main character from our video, named Bud. We created posters that looked like real movie posters complete with directors, actors, and studio information and the phrase "coming to a computer near you this summer." We teased the employees for two months before the release of the new version with our "Bud Gets Wiser" campaign to get them excited about it. They really knew nothing more than what the poster said. We did not tell them it was a new selling process. We did not tell them it was a computer-based program (first ever for the company), and we did not tell them dates, times or any other detail. We just got them excited that something special was going to happen. The result, a 95% attendance, and graduation (passed all tests with an 80% or better) rate. Now, that's exciting!

In my journeys, I have found many companies try this through T-shirts or ornaments for the employee's desk, etc. There are many ways to do this, but the purpose of the marketing is to enforce and enhance the culture. Make sure this is the case.

The key to a good marketing campaign is that it must fit your culture. For some of you, this play on words and the movie poster genre may be too cutesy for your culture. Remember that Everything Speaks!

Another great idea you can try is the University Spirit Week. Each year, we would stage a spirit week on each of our campuses around the country. The intent was to raise the level of awareness of the university and its benefit to the employees. Each campus staged events during the week to bring attention to the university. We even spiced it up and had a contest between the campuses on who could do the most creative and effective University Spirit Week. Activities associated with this included:

- Providing box lunches one day to anyone who attended the "What your university can do for you" luncheon.
- Special days and outings during the week recognizing the degree earners.
- Lapel pins given to each degree earner in a special ceremony.
- Contest among the different colleges including Olympic-style competition.
- Skits and other types of acting during meetings for exposure.
- Dress-up days for the employees.
- College Sweatshirt day where everyone wears their favorite sweatshirt.

Campus Life

This is the one that most companies overlook when building their corporate university. All traditional universities expend lots of energy trying to create energy on their campus. This can be done in many ways from the student centers to the extra-curricular activities like drama or sports, to the fraternities and sororities. All of these things are added to the traditional university for one reason – to create a lifestyle on the campus and to focus on the person as a whole, not just as a student.

I am not suggesting that you start participating in interscholastic sports leagues or your company put on "The Tempest" this fall, but I am suggesting that this is a very important part of your corporate university. This is where the culture's people side comes together with the process side. The process obviously is the training in your corporate university. Providing a solid campus life cares for the people side.

When we refer to the campus, we are using the term loosely since a Type IV university is not based in a building, but rather at the point of contact in the field. So I am not describing things you would only do at your training center. I am describing things that should be done throughout the company. Your entire staff should be in a constant improvement mode. It's required in today's pace of technology and competition.

The Japanese have a word for this, kaizen. Kaizen is translated as **a constant improvement**. This is the model that they use in all of their business. When they create something, they spend their efforts improving it while they look for the next breakthrough. No two model years pass in Japan with the same product being offered. This is almost the opposite of America, where the same model may be in place for three or four years while we look for the next big breakthrough. Ken Blanchard in his book, Mission Possible, describes this process in more detail when he suggests dividing your company into two concurrent teams – one focusing on improving the present and one focusing on improving the future.

For your culture, kaizen means that everyone is constantly improving himself or herself through your corporate university. But, if we follow traditional training logic, the university would only be responsible for making people "process smart." In other words, the people side of the culture gets ignored. After all, we can't measure it, and with the training budget being the first thing to get cut every time there is trouble, why would the training people want to get into this area? Who could blame them?

But for most companies, this part of an employee's life goes unnoticed and undeveloped. Only the strong, self-motivated will survive, and they will do so whether you help them or not. In building an experience culture, you need every person pulling the same weight all the time. This means preparing them to be successful both process wise and people wise.

Another great idea we picked up was when a campus created "fratorities." These were fraternity-like clubs that were based on the colleges. Each college had its own fratority - so named because it had both male and female members. The fratorities were each given a room in the building to use as their "house." They got some small funds to decorate their houses, but mostly the employees brought in stuff from their homes. These houses served as the break room for the employees. They stirred some healthy competition among the employees. One word of caution, though; segregating like this could do more harm than good depending on your current culture. **Run it through your experience formula first.**

The answer to the fifth element of a Learning corporate university is really a segue into our next chapter because it deals with issues going beyond training but still connected. This is where you start to build your bridge—linking training to job description—meaning everyone attends, everyone learns, and everyone gains.

Your corporate university must make sure all five of these elements are in place if you wish to have the impact of kaizen. Even if you try to cut corners on some of these ideas in this chapter, you will still be successful because any part of this will help make you better. There is a reason this is the second longest chapter in this book. I feel that the establishing of a corporate university is the key to providing the proper "programming" of your experience culture.

Think of it this way, if Steve Jobs had focused on building a better Walkman would we have the iPod? Go big.

Reflections

What are the most important takeaways you got from this chapter?

Make a list of challenges (opportunities) you see in implementing a Learning University in your organization.

Who else in your organization needs to read this?

Awards and Recognition

People don't do things stupid on purpose.

Now that's an opening quote. But before you do any work on your awards and recognition program, you must accept this principle. What do I mean by this? Well, this discussion is appropriate for any company whether it's going through a culture change or not.

People (employees especially) don't do things stupid on purpose. "Now wait a minute," you're saying, "You have never met some of my employees!" Okay, fair enough, but make sure that you are reading this statement correctly.

I am not saying your employees won't do stupid things; I am saying that they won't do them on purpose. It is never their intention to be stupid or do stupid things; it just sort of happens – to all of us! At the time the employee makes a decision and takes action, it makes total sense to them – they thought it was a good idea. Later, he or she may look back and see that it was not such a great decision.

Need proof? Go to your local mall this weekend and notice some of the interesting clothing on some of the people. Notice the way some people adorn themselves decoratively. Haven't you ever asked yourself, "Why would you pierce that?" or "Why would you wear those shoes with that dress?" No matter how unmatched or uncoordinated someone's wardrobe may be to you, at some point and time in that person's day, he got up, got dressed and stood in front of the mirror and said, "Looking good!" In other words, he meant to dress that way! She meant to wear those shoes!

These people did not get up and say, "Hey, I wonder how stupid I could look today?" They got up and said, "This looks good!" Now later, the lady with the shoes may catch a glimpse of herself walking by a mirror and say, "What was I thinking when I put these shoes on?" She now realizes that what she did was not so smart, but that was not her intention.

The best example of this is my dad. Every Sunday morning while I was growing up, there was a ritual in our household when my father would come out of the bedroom sporting the most not-matching or gaudy tie we had ever seen. Now, I guarantee you that he hated having to change his tie (which we made him do almost every time.) He tried desperately to put together a coordinated outfit to avoid the public ridicule of his family. My father never intended to be "stupid" in his dress; he's just fashion challenged.

People never intend to make stupid decisions or behave stupidly, although you may sometimes swear that this is true. You must practice patience and be careful that you do not misinterpret someone's behavior as resistance to the culture.

The frustrating part of this is when you confront employees after they have done something stupid. (Please keep in mind that I am using the term stupid here light-heartedly – for humor. I do not mean to offend.) What is their response? You ask them, "Why did you do this?" or more commonly you will ask, "What were you thinking?" And they respond, "I don't know." Frustrating though it is, they are telling you the truth! They really don't know. At the time they made the decision, it made perfectly good sense. Later they look back on it and wonder why they did it that way.

You are no different. Aren't there things in your life you look back on now and say, **"What was I thinking?"** And you answer yourself, "I have no idea." If you need to jog your memory, just grab your high school yearbook. I'm sure there is a picture or two there to remind you and help you grasp this principle. So, give your employees the benefit of the doubt here and never write someone off too early or overreact.

Why is this principle so important? Because you are designing an **experience culture**. What is one of the outcomes you are looking for from your new culture? Increased customer care and compassion. In the early stages, you will have a lot of employees (hourly and salary) who will make decisions for your company that will turn out bad. Their intent was to follow the lead of your new culture and be "of service" to the customer and provide a remarkable experience.

Sometimes, they will ignore or forget about your experience formula and give away the farm. Your natural tendency will be to reprimand them and let them have it. Be very careful! (Remember, the experience formula is based on three essential elements—employees, customers, and stakeholders.)

Your employees are looking for a reason **not** to change. The culture has worked fine for them up to this point, and they do not understand why it needs to change. And if you are one of those "good" companies Jim Collins talks about in his book Good to Great, then they will embrace the current culture.

If the first time they attempt to change and do what they think you are asking and you beat them down for it, you have just pushed them to the resistance side (see "Getting to the Heart of the Matter" on page 302.) In other words, you have just "programmed" the culture the wrong direction! Keep this principle in mind at all times when managing your culture change. If you are trying to instill an experience culture, then be focuses on the experience of your employees – **the employee experience is as important as the customer experience.**

The culture cycle of culture change starts with programming and ends with behavior. The behavior you see demonstrated by employees is a direct result of the chain reaction of the programming they have received. In the last example, the programming took you in the wrong direction. So, how do you take the programming in the right direction? One great way is a strong awards and recognition program.

We all know that **what gets rewarded gets repeated** (since you read it so many times already in this book #programming) and awards are a form of programming the culture. But are there some rules to follow when awarding in an experience culture? Absolutely.

First, two more principles. These are borrowed from Ferdinand Fournies' book, Coaching for Improved Work Performance.

1.   **All behavior is rewarded.** Your non-action says just as much about your people as your reaction. If you are like most companies, there is definite favoritism at play in your departments, especially in a sales organization.

It is very typical for the top performers in a company to get by with more than the lower performers. See if this story sounds like your company.

One of your managers is holding a meeting scheduled to start at 9 a.m. At 9:12 a.m. the star performer for the department walks in late. The manager welcomes him and tells him he is glad that he made it. At 9:16 a.m. the non-star performer walks in and the manager proceeds to let them have it. An ensuing lecture about responsibility and the importance of being on time takes place.

Sound familiar? What has just happened here? Well, **all** of the behavior was just rewarded. Not just the two who came in late, but everyone. What do I mean? The star performer was rewarded for being late because no action was taken against him when he was. The manager just rewarded that behavior you ask? You bet. He did nothing that seemed to reward it, but his condoning of the behavior just programmed the star performer that his behavior was okay – that it was acceptable.

Second, the non-star's behavior was rewarded. Granted his reward was a lecture and reprimand, but he deserved it. If the meeting is to start at 9 a.m., then everyone must be there. The non-star knows that being late was wrong. His behavior was rewarded (with the booby prize), and he was programmed.

Last, but certainly not least, the other employees at the meeting had their behavior rewarded or at least programmed. They now see that the culture is one that says, "If you are performing or sales are up or are the boss' favorite, you can get away with stuff and don't have to follow the rules. But don't let your sales go down or you have had it." **Is this the message you want to be sent through your culture change cycle?**

Many times, managers base their reaction to an offense on what they are feeling or what they are doing at that time. We often think to ourselves, "I don't have time to mess with this right now." Keep this in mind, though. If you let someone come in late to work and choose not to say anything, you have just **rewarded their behavior** and programmed them that it is okay.

"That's not fair," you say. "The rules are obvious, and the employee knows better than to be late. If I don't say anything, I'm not telling him it's okay." Oh, really? Have you ever delayed a report due because you knew the boss went out of town on an unscheduled trip for three days – the day your report was due? We have all tried to get away with whatever we could. The difference here is that if the employee knows that you know, and you choose not to act, he or she will take this as a sign of condoning from you and the behavior will continue because it was "rewarded." When you confront the employee about it after the fourth or fifth time, he or she will look at you bewildered. If it was such a big deal, why didn't you bring it up before? Pretty compelling argument.

2.   **Reward only those who meet your standards**. You must recognize all efforts to get better by your employees, but do not give them the prize until they have truly earned it.

This one is hard to do, especially for your "people" managers. When someone gets so close to the bar, you just have to give it to him or her, don't you? You know who you are. But think about what you are doing. If you tell your children they can go to the zoo if they get an A, but then let them go anyway when they get a B because you saw them study hard, you are doing them a disservice. Why?

Because you have just rewarded their behavior and, in so doing, programmed them that the effort is all that counts. In the service industry, we get no points with the customer for effort. We get points for results. Period. Do not let your employees think that close is good enough. Once they start to believe this, it becomes a belief of your culture, and you know what that means…

If you have a contest and no one gets to the level of productivity or performance you set, then no one wins. This is a sign that you set the bar too high. To give someone a prize just to save your face is again programming the culture in the wrong way.

You must use the experience formula when creating contests, incentives, and awards for your company.

If you do this, there should be no reason the example above would ever happen (although it does).

The Rules of Awards

When creating your awards and recognition program, try to follow these guidelines (rules):

- There should be an award from each part of the business – one from the customer, one from the business (management) and one from the employees. The third one is the hardest since most people turn these into popularity contests.
- Involve the employees in the awards program process.
- The awards program must include three time periods – annual, monthly, and "at the moment it happens."
- All awards programs have the shelf life of milk.
- The award must fit the behavior.
- The award must be for doing more than is expected.
- The awards must be public.

- The awards must be evenly distributed between on-stage (direct customer contact) employees and backstage (i.e. operations) employees.
- Theme the awards with your culture's language.
- Make the awards program part of your promotion process.
- Do not confuse recognition and reinforcement skills as part of your awards process.

Let's examine each of these guidelines.

Rule 1. There should be an award from each part of the business.

Most award programs come from the top down. This is traditional management style and traditional culture style. But you are building an experience culture, and this requires awards from three places – customers, management, and peers.

Examine your evaluation cards in your business. Are they evaluations of your company or your employees? Remember, if you are benchmarking yourself, you will only be better than yourself, which may be worse than the competition. Evaluation cards are one of the first things we look at in a company. They tell us so much about the company. They are usually too long, measure too openly and provide no data the company can use. Most importantly, though, they rarely ask for feedback on the employees.

Your awards and recognition program must seek to solicit awards. What do we mean by that? If the key to changing your culture is through programming the cycle, then you must design a program (the process half of a culture) to give you as much opportunity to "program" your employees (the people side of the culture) in the right ways as possible. The more comment cards you can get from your customer that mention individuals, the more impact you will have. When a client recognizes an employee, it usually means more to them than when their boss does.

One thing to be careful about here is the backstage employee in your company. Make sure that you design ways to solicit customer input for the "back stagers" as well. This group is usually treated as seconds to the on-stage group anyway. An awards program that gives more recognition to the on-stage than it does to the backstage will not develop an experience culture. Some companies will have the on-stage award winner select the backstage person who helped them the most to also receive the award.

Social media has become a remarkable way to recognize employees. Happy customers often tell their friends online. Make sure you are monitoring this activity, so you can call it out and acknowledge and reward the employee mentioned in the tweet or post.

Second, have a recognition program for your employees to recognize each other. In more than one company, we have implemented a program called "Hero Stars." These are brightly colored, peel-and-stick awards that can be worn by the person who won it for everyone to see. This award was given to an employee who went above and beyond the call of duty either in service to a customer or in service to another employee.

The second scenario (a fellow employee) is the powerful part of this award. When one employee says to another, "Hey, you were a hero" it makes an impact. We have seen employees wear these stars for days. Every employee in the company knows what it means and respects it more because it came from a peer, not from kissing up to management.

This award program extends into management as well, though. The beauty of this program was that it also satisfied part of the third guideline above – an award for "in the moment." These Hero Stars are easy because they do not have to be ordered. You can keep stacks of them in your desk drawer ready to go at all times. A side note on this program. When I first tried it, we used our own computer-generated forms. The employees were not too thrilled with a piece of form paper run through a laser printer. But this brightly colored, professionally printed award meant a lot. They became competitive trying to earn a Hero Star. This programming of the culture was wonderful, and it paid off marvelously. The employees were competitive about working harder and providing more and better service!

The last award types are your typical management or business awards. These are the ones set and given by management. Whether you call them the "People's Choice" awards or not, since they are from management, they will always seem this way. The best advice with these types of awards is to make sure they have tangible criteria for winning. Factual numbers, increases in percentages, etc., are all examples of taking this award from a popularity contest to an honor.

Rule 2. Involve the employees in the awards program process.

This is an important point and one that I will give you help with in the next chapter. We have always been taught that people support and give greater effort to causes they had a part in creating. The same applies to your awards program. The tendency in a hierarchical managed company will be to put two or three managers on a committee and let them come up with it. Use the Culture Council described in the next chapter. By now, you have probably realized you will need all the help you can get to make this change work.

Rule 3. The awards program must include awards from three time periods.

The more often you can give awards the better, right? Well, not entirely. Employees don't do things stupid on purpose and neither should you. Having a ceremony every other day to give out awards dilutes their importance in the minds of your employees and therefore weakens their impact. Have a balanced awards program to cover three time periods – annually, monthly and in the moment.

The annual awards program should be the crème de la crème of your awards. They should be the biggest and nicest prizes since they are used to recognize a goal for a full year of performance. But since they only come once a year, their effectiveness in programming your culture is minimal. You need more immediate feedback to change behavior.

Monthly awards help to accomplish the programming power of your awards program. They also increase the chances for people to win. You will have twelve winners for each monthly award and only one for each annual.

Lastly, have a part of your awards process that can happen whenever. We call this the "as it happens" award. These awards have no specific time periods tied to them. They can be immediate and powerful. They are very involved in the programming of your culture, more so than the other two time periods.

Rule 4. All award programs have the shelf life of milk.

You must constantly look for new ways to reward your performers. The older an award gets, the less "Pow" it has. This is to say, the longer you give out a certain award, and the more people will win it and the less special it will become.

The satisfied feeling of accomplishment that you will get from winning this award will expire in 7 days.

There are some exceptions to this, like your traditional awards tied to your folklore or your annual sales or service awards, but the rest must be kept fresh.

Rule 5. The award must fit the behavior.

This is very common. We have this neat hoo-ha that just came into our possession, and we decide to give it to the employees. So we design a quickie contest or worse yet, just arbitrarily on our infinite wisdom declare a winner of the prize.

An award is an award, whether it is a trophy, free meal, or Hero Star; at least that is the way your employees see it. It is very common for management to think that what motivated them will motivate others. We often forget that is why we are management, and they are not.

It relates back to guideline two above in that the annual award should be larger and the behavior that must be performed to win it must also be **greater and consistent over a longer period**. Something that was relatively easy to accomplish should have a small reward and something awesome should have the awesome award attached to it.

In the case of the example above, try to establish in your culture a sharing of the award resources among the different departments. This way, a last-minute award can be used to its full potential. If a person is given a cool award for doing something average, they will feel awkward about it, and it can alienate them from the rest of their peers. They know that their peers know that this accomplishment was a rather ordinary accomplishment and doesn't fit the reward so that it will diminish the impact. Have you ever seen anyone feel guilty about receiving an award? They usually try to share it with the whole team, but then that makes the team feel bad because they feel guilty for making the winner feel guilty, and so on, and so on. (This is beginning to sound like a script from a sitcom.)

Rule 6.   The award must be for doing more than is expected.

Earlier, rule #2 said, "Reward only those who meet your expectations." This will only work when your expectations are higher than normal. You are trying to cultivate an experience culture, and in so doing you are trying to make **exceeding people's expectations** second nature to your employees.

In a recent survey conducted trying to find the effects of service recovery, the researchers came across the following interesting statistics. Service recovery is how we handle a customer problem once it has been brought to our attention. In the survey, they found that depending on how well the complaint was handled would determine whether or not the company would ever get another shot at that customer's business. The survey found that if the company's handling of the complaint:

> **The survey found that if the company's handling of the complaint:**
>
> Did not meet customer's expectations
> *12% would buy again*
>
> Met the customer's expectations
> *46% would buy again*
>
> Exceeded the customer's expectations
> *86% would buy again*

What a dramatic difference is proven through this research. If your employees don't do their jobs, then you have very little chance of ever seeing them again – no surprise. If they do their jobs and meet the customer's expectations, then you have a much greater chance. But even if you take care of their problem to the customer's expectation and satisfaction, you still loose over 50%! Your company cannot afford that.

Why the tough numbers? Why do we get a less than 50/50 chance to see a customer again if we meet their expectations? (By the way, we have conducted similar research in retail and have found that this 50/50 chance is true even on the front end. In other words, not when they have a problem, but when they first buy.)

Our post-digital world has left customers an infinite number of options. If my local company cannot satisfy me, I will just go online. Forrester completed a study last Fall of Millennial shoppers. They found that over 60% still preferred to shop in a brick and mortar store, but they usually shop online. Why? Because the experience in the store did not exceed their expectations. And in today's online world, why would I get out of my pajamas and leave my house if the experience is no different?

Online has changed the face of business – no matter what your product or service is. People (foolishly) believe that **if they read it online, it must be true!**

With this being the case, the only way you will get to the next level is if you set the bar at the next level for your employees. Think back to the visible and unvisible exercise you did in Chapter One. If you are looking for where to set the bar…need I say more?

A word of caution, though. Your mighty warrior employees are not ready to "be the bar." They need time to get there. Make sure your bar is not so far over their heads that they cannot see it or reach it. Nothing is more demoralizing than being put in a "no-win" situation.

Rule 7.   The awards must be public.

If you want to have any impact at all on your employee's behavior, you must make sure that as much of your awarding is done in public as possible. You may have some shy ones on your team, but believe me, they are the ones who will take that certificate or Hero Star home and keep it on their wall for the rest of their lives.

An award given in public dramatically adds to the impact. We are all in competition with each other as humans, and we love it when others see us as the "winner." A good experience culture gets its people together at least once (best do twice) a month to share the news of the business. Make the awards part of this time.

Keep a special bulletin board reserved just for bragging. It should be full of pictures of your heroes, letters from management and feedback from customers or guests. NEVER be afraid to display negative feedback from your customers. It is how you grow. Try to do it in a positive light. Put headings on the board that read "THUMBS UP" and "THUMBS DOWN," or use Disney's "Good Show – Bad Show" rating system. Even my city's local paper publishes a monthly CHEERS AND JEERS section to highlight outstanding and not-so-outstanding public deeds.

Rule 8. The awards must be evenly distributed between on-stage performers and backstage performers.

This is soooo hard to do because the on-stage or "customer contact" employees make it easy on you. They have sales numbers and customer letters galore – an easy way to track accomplishment. In almost every case I had studied before an experience culture was put into place, the awards program was distributed 90% on-stage and the obligatory 10% included "Did Not Kill Anyone with a Forklift Safety Award" award for backstage.

Get creative. Look for ways to award the performance of your backstage employees. **Try to maintain a balance.** You will always have more on-stage awards than backstage awards because there are usually more employees on-stage. Just keep the margin of the difference small.

Rule 9. Theme the awards with your culture's language.

On one of the early stops of this journey, you were given the assignment to create your company's new language and vocabulary. If you have themed your culture after a movie studio, then obviously you would want to give out "Oscars." If you have themed your culture after a sports team, then you would have the MVP award and so on. This part of the process makes perfect sense; it is just overlooked so often!

Rule 10. Make the awards program part of your promotion process.

What is the value in winning all the awards if your peers get the promotion? Make the award more than just a plaque. Add incentive by directly linking your awards program to your promotion process. Make one of the criteria for promotion in your company winning a certain number of Hero Stars or other awards that you have created.

Rule 11. Do not confuse recognition and reinforcement skills as part of your awards process.

We have used the terms award and reward interchangeably in this chapter simply because they are interchangeable. When you look in the American Heritage Dictionary (last time, promise), you will see that the definitions are almost the same. When you look in the thesaurus, each word is listed for the other. Now that's interchangeable.

But the term recognition and award do have different meanings. Recognition is defined as (I don't have to tell you from where) "attention or favorable notice." There is great power in showing attention to the behavior of your employees. **This is the best way to "program" them and your culture.**

Recognition is not limited to a trophy or certificate. It is made up of the less tangible like the hard-to-pry "thank you" out of a manager. As a leader, one of your key skills is your ability to recognize and reinforce positive behavior to fit your culture. The beauty of this skill is that it does not have to meet all the guidelines above. It never waits for a ceremony. It does not require a plaque. And it happens at the same time as the behavior (at the moment) – a major point.

Here is the rule for the difference between an award or reward and recognition:

Use the recognition to acknowledge behavior and use the award to acknowledge results.

Here is a list of some simple recognition ideas that you can give employees every day, no waiting!

1. Say thank you (and mean it!)
2. Atta boy notes (handwritten by you, not your secretary and not in email!)
3. Send someone to a strategy meeting in your place.
4. Introduce your employees and peers to management and brag about their great work.
5. Consult with a high performer on a problem or issue telling him you value his opinion because of his behavior.
6. Write "thank you" or other quick notes on your business card.
7. Cover for them while they take an extra break.
8. Ask other people to comment to the person on your behalf.
9. Arrange for them to have lunch with Mr. Big.
10. Give them an afternoon off with pay.
11. Give them a two-hour lunch instead of one hour.
12. Pass on positive comments you get on the employee from others to them as soon as you hear it.
13. Give them a library afternoon to go and play on the Internet.
14. Keep a whiteboard on the wall to write your comments as you see a positive behavior happening.
15. Be at the front lines to see it happen.

This last one is critical. Too much of the awards and recognition given out in companies today are by people who never even saw it happen. It's like letting the minister who never met your cousin perform the eulogy – empty and fake. We could go on for hours about the importance of you being on the front lines, but hey, there are 3,000 other books out there to discuss that. Besides, this is one of those topics where you know what is right; you're just not doing it!

Secret Shopping

One of the best ways to support an awards and recognition program is through the use of a secret or mystery shopping program. When I was a COO for a footwear retailer, we had a practice of hiring companies to "secret shop" our stores. They would come in the store and make a purchase with a video camera hidden on their person. We would watch the videos and **award great performances** and then correct poor ones. Unfortunately, we seemed to have many poorer ones than good ones each month.

While the idea of a small video camera was totally "spy" a few years ago, today **everyone has a video camera** on their mobile device. And anyone can secret shop your business. There are still several secret or mystery shopping services out there, and all are solid in their deliverables. The problem is the cost. For most independent businesses, it is too expensive a tool to use. In fact, even when I was using it back in the day, we limited it to four of our fourteen stores a month due to the cost.

So, how do you get the terrific feedback of a secret shopper without the expense of a service or company? Simple, use your network. You have family and friends and colleagues who would all be happy to serve. And you can trust what they say to be genuine and not "trumped up."

When I had my retail stores, I used to have my customers do the secret shopping. They could send in a friend of theirs who had not been in before and then fill out a survey of their experience. The "friend" got a gift card (to a coffee shop in town, not our store) and the customer who recruited them and sent them to "shop" us got a gift card (for our store.) We even had a gift card for the shopper to use when they bought, so it never cost them anything. So each one of these secret shops cost us $100 versus several hundred. I was the only one who could initiate and approve, so I could control how many happened each month. We took money out of our advertising budget to pay for this and tried to shop each store one to two times per month.

The key to a secret shop, though, is in the questions you are asking. Drive through any fast food lane today, and you will probably get a receipt with a phone number for a survey on the bottom. I have used services like this in the past and can honestly say that the data served *me* more than the customer. In other words, I got excited because I was looking at numbers and data on paper, but the data really did not help me improve the business. Sure, the data showed some indicators, but what you need are examples.

Employees do not respond to "customer satisfaction %'s." Those are just numbers on a page. What they need are real examples to back up the numbers. Remember, the **definition of learning** is a *change in behavior*. What your employees need is examples of **why** the score is what it is (high or low.) An employee cannot change his or her behavior if they do not know what specifically you are looking for; that was what was great about those videos from my shoe days. Employees could see themselves in action (or not in action as the case might have been) and when we told them they got a 75 out of 100, they immediately wanted to know why. With the video, I could show them why.

So, if you are going to use secret shoppers, you need to make sure they give you specific examples of what they liked, loved and did not like or love in your store. Have them focus on the "**experience**" in your store or with your company. After all, that is what builds brands faster than anything. Don't have them fill out a form with ratings (1 to 5) without giving you a specific example for each rating. (By the way, if you use a rating system, make sure it is 1 to 7 and not 1 to 5. With 1 to 5 systems, you will get a lot of 3's which do not tell you anything. Use a rating scale that forces the customer to tell you good or bad and not okay or average.

You may not be a retailer, but these secret shopping principles can apply to any business that has customers. And they can be a big help in programing your culture the right way to provide an experience.

Most traditional cultures have the "programming" that people are paid to do a job, and that should be good enough. In other words, that's their reward - a paycheck. I remember a sign that used to hang in an office I once visited that said, "I am not here to tell you what you are doing right. I am here to tell you what you are doing wrong!" If this is yours or your or your company's motto, you have a lot of work to do.

Nothing could be further from the truth. In an experience culture, you are looking at all times to catch people doing things right. Does this mean that we ignore the bad? Absolutely not! **The only way to get better is to deal with the negative performances**. But you will get considerably deeper and much quicker results from giving them kudos when they do right than you will by giving them "written notices" when they do wrong. This gives you a chance to recognize them for it, and we said earlier "what gets rewarded gets repeated." Eventually, the "exceeding the customer's expectations" mentality will weave its way into the fabric of your culture and find its seat on the bus to the Culturrific! Experience team.

One company we worked with created its own culture police. These "police" were given tickets to pass out to the employees when they caught them – doing something right! The employees could redeem the tickets for merchandise or concessions in the break room. These culture police put a positive spin on the hall monitor of old. When you make people feel good about what they are doing, you are practicing one of the six Principles of Learning: The Principle of Effect, which says, **"learning accompanied by a satisfied feeling of accomplishment is dramatically more effective."** When we make them feel good about their accomplishment, they learn from it and when they learn from it – they and the culture have been programmed! Help your people not to do things stupid on purpose. You've set the stage, now award the performances.

Reflections

What are the most important takeaways you got from this chapter?

What are the best parts and worst parts of your current awards and recognition program?

Who else in your organization needs to read this and help you re-engineer?

Create a Culture Council

Never underestimate the power of a few motivated employees to change your culture for good.

The Culture Council can be an intricate part of each corporate university and your awards and recognition program. Its stretch reaches far beyond that of training and seeks to capture the hearts and heads of the employees of your company. It is an organization made up of people from all levels of your company—management, hourly, and executive levels - with the purpose of keeping the culture alive and creating continuous enthusiasm throughout the company for both the employee and the customer.

In a previous chapter, I stated that the purpose of the Culture Council was to provide for the development of the people side of your culture. One of the many obstacles facing management when it tries a culture shift is that there is so much to be done and so little resources. There are four major reasons to create a Culture Council within your company.

1. **To increase your resources**. By involving your hourly employees, you free up management's time to focus on your customer. How much time do your managers spend focusing on the customer right now? Do you want to implement a new program like this to make that timeless? Hopefully, you are answering this question by saying that your experience formula dictates that you need a council like this to be successful.

2.	**To connect your people side with the process side.**
This is a very hard thing to do in culture change. It's
not a new or startling idea to involve your hourly or
frontline people in the process. As a matter of fact,
when we speak to companies about their cultures, the
president or senior executive we are dealing with
shares this with us even before we bring it up.
Unfortunately, many companies feel they have met
this criterion by inviting some select hourly people to
a strategy session during the Design Phase of the
culture change outlined in earlier chapters of this
book. The time you need the hourly employees the
most is when you start changing their lives.

They must be involved if you expect any success. The
Culture Council is a proven method for gaining their
involvement on an ongoing basis.

3.	**To keep the initiative alive (kaizen).** Too many
culture changes fail because they quickly turn into the
flavor-of-the-month programs. When management
tries to do it all, it soon finds there are more pressing
needs to attend to, and it slowly but surely will take its
foot off of the gas pedal of the culture change bus. The
members of this group still include management, but
it is a representative of management, not all of the
management that physically works with this group.
This person must change every few months so they
can keep their customer focus alive as well.

4.	**There are many "campus life" activities and
communications that need to happen in your
company.** The Culture Council, as you will see, is
responsible for keeping the employees informed and
active in the culture. Imagine the power of having all

of your employees focused on changing the culture instead of a committee.

The Culture Council gives employees a chance to interact and discuss the challenges and concerns them and their peers are having within their departments as well as throughout the company. But above all, it's a fun way for employees to stay involved with and uphold the culture. The council idea was born from the purpose statement and ensures that you are staying true to each element of your experience formula.

What if I'm a Small Company?

This chapter is written and focused on larger organizations, I'll admit. The majority of companies that I work with have been larger in size when it comes to a number of employees. But I have never let the size of a company dictate the need for a Culture Council.

If you are a small business with one location and 12 employees, you can still use the idea of a Culture Council to drive your experience culture. You simply follow the principles and not the structure outlined in this next section. What you are about to read is what I have learned from best practices of Culture Councils I have witnessed.

So, small business entrepreneurs, read the rest of this chapter and look for the principles. There is no need to develop an overly complicated structure. It may be just two people and more of a committee than a council. But make sure someone (multiple someone's) own the responsibility of keeping your culture alive. It doesn't take much to derail your culture change. You need all the help you can get.

How to build the Council (medium or larger business)

You will need at least two managers—one from an on-stage (or front of the house) department and one from backstage (back of the house)—and at least one executive who are willing and available to meet twice a month and act as facilitators for the council. They are not in charge, but you will need someone present to help with approvals on decisions and offer advice and input to make sure all sides of an issue are heard and understood. These employees must understand the role they are playing. They are responsible for making sure the Culture Council uses good judgment in all its decisions and they stay within the bounds of their authority. It is very hard for the employees to adjust to different leadership, so make sure the management people chosen to serve can meet the time commitment and requirements of the position.

You will also need to caution these management representatives of your council not to get too involved running the council. Their role is simply advisory. They should not make decisions or head committees. It defeats the purpose of the Culture Council. You are looking to seed the values of your culture with a grass roots effort when you create a Culture Council. Let the grassroots people run it.

Decide how your representation will be patterned for your Culture Council. The perfect world would be to have a representative from each department, but you want to be careful not to have 100 people on this council. We all know what it is like to work with a team that large. Decisions and execution are cumbersome and often worthless. You may decide to create "districts" inside your company to group departments with similar responsibilities to lower the total number on your council.

Now comes the fun part—picking and electing the council representatives. This process can be done many different ways, but we have found that an election is the best way to get representatives on your council who care and will work for you. The Culture Council members' time is only on the clock during their twice-a-month meetings. All other time spent on this endeavor will be "on their own." This ensures you are following Disney's Quality Business Practices philosophy. It also gains you employees who are dedicated to your cause. How do you measure dedication? Volunteerism.

Have the employees petition to represent their department by completing a "platform" paper they acquire from your Casting office. (This used to be your HR office; hopefully you are keeping up.) This platform should be a paper answering a series of questions on why they would be good to represent their department and what talents or skills they bring to the table. You can even have some real fun with this and have the candidates give speeches in your employee cafeteria during lunch or dinner on select days.

If more than one employee applies from each department, then the employees will campaign for a position on the council, and the best candidate will be chosen by an open election in the company. You can let this be an event for your company by having the employees create buttons or posters or campaign slogans for their platform. Stage an Election Day and have everyone vote when they pick up their paycheck (or at a common exit or elevator). The key is to make sure that being on this council is an honor for the employee. One they will work extremely hard for.

Decide on a time span for serving on the Culture Council before the election. The recommended time is six months since it takes a while to get this rolling and many activities require months of planning.

Once your council has been chosen, the members will meet bi-monthly for a minimum of one hour to discuss events, culture issues, customer issues, weekend meetings, and any relative information to carry over the monthly business.

Stay with the "student government" mentality everyone remembers from school and have organized offices on your council. You don't want to add to much structure to this (written right before we give you more structure.) *The following ideas are if you have a large one site company with lots of people wanting to serve.* Do not add officers unless your Culture Council is over 15 people.

- President: Presiding officer who serves as an ex officio member of the Council. It is the responsibility of the president to uphold parliamentary procedures during the meeting and to coordinate and schedule Culture Council meetings through the preparation of notices and agendas of all meetings.

- VP of Internal Affairs: It is the responsibility of this officer to coordinate and chair all committees responsible for internal activities and affairs of your company. This includes parties, sporting events, and leagues and any other contest or activities designed solely for internal participation. This officer is dedicated to enhancing the employee experience the people side of your culture.

- VP of External Affairs: It is the responsibility of this officer to coordinate and chair all committees responsible for external activities of your company. In keeping with an experience culture's values and principles, it is very important to be involved in community relations and activities that give back to the community. These activities may include fund-raisers, canned food drives, etc. This officer is also dedicated to upholding the customer experience.

- VP of Communication: It is the responsibility of this officer to coordinate and serve as editor of your internal company newsletter. One great way to keep the culture alive is through strong communication among the entire cast. This person also maintains any communication bulletin boards like the ones mentioned in this book. This officer makes sure this happens.

- VP of Finance: It is the responsibility of this officer to maintain the books and budget for all of the Council's activities. This officer also sparks creativity through unique fundraising activities of the Culture Council. Your Council will need a budget to be successful, but they can also raise some of their funds themselves.

- VP of Awards and Recognition: It is the responsibility of this officer to administer and facilitate the award/recognition programs of your company. This person must make sure all award nominations are collected; votes are tabulated, awards printed and presented at your company's all-employee meetings.

- Scribe: This officer maintains the notes and accounts of each Culture Council meeting. A typed report of these "minutes" must be completed and submitted to the president and the Casting department of your company and read at the start of each meeting.

In addition to these officers and the actual Culture Council members, feel free to have other employees volunteer to be on different committees for more involvement. Having a Culture Council does not mean that everyone else is exempt or cannot participate. The Council is a guiding body of employees, which will still need lots of help from the employee base of your company.

Now you may be thinking, so you want me to replace my company's VP of Communication with a front-line employee? No, not exactly. Keep in mind that the nature of the Culture Council is directly proportionate to the size and locations of your company.

If you have a small company with everyone working in one building, then you will have one Culture Council. But if you have 300 locations, it is conceivable that you could have 300 Culture Councils. How hard is it for you in the large company to get the "message" out? Sometimes impossible. Now, what if you had a dedicated team of people at the front lines of each location making it happen for you? Now that is synergy.

The basic rule here would be to use the number of employees in the location to make your decision. For example, if you have 300 locations and each location has 300 people, then you need 300 Culture Councils. But if you have 300 locations each with 10 people, then you would be better do construct your Councils on a district or regional level. ALWAYS have one for the corporate or home office. These people need it more than anyone.

Budget Time and their Money

The Culture Council will need a budget and must be expected to maintain it like a profit and loss statement. This group must still act and think like a service business since that is what your company is.

One of the pitfalls of this group is it may tend to think of themselves as the social committee. While social events are one of its agenda items, it is far from the only one. As you see from the officers listed above, the Culture Council will be responsible for much more. Your Culture Council pulls together several functions, which currently may be split throughout your company. It is funny that when re-engineering takes place, we rarely, if ever, re-engineer our employee programs and processes.

The Culture Council ties together the following functions into one group. Your new experience culture is cross-departmental with no walls between the different parts of your company. These functions help to serve that purpose.

1. The company newsletter. Yes, you may already have a wonderful four-color, 75-page newsletter. We are not suggesting you start over (unless you really do have a four-color 75-page newsletter!) We are suggesting that this function must become part of your Culture Council. Again, if you are the 300 location/300 employees per Location Company, then you need a newsletter for each location in addition to the "Big News from the Ivory Tower" version.

2. The monthly all-employee meetings. How often are your employees getting together to celebrate victory and discuss shortcomings? What issues are facing your customers? Who knows this? Your frontline employees who serve on the council. They can get the word out better than any press agency.

3. The awards and recognition programs. Again, you may have a whole department dedicated to this topic, but the VP of Awards and Recognition must be on the Culture Council. They may certainly be the one already in charge of awards and recognition of your company. NOTE: This Council is not responsible for sales promotions or other incentive programs for your company. These should remain in the care of the ones who deal with it now. They should seek advice from the Council, but there are many legal implications with these types of programs, and you must be careful.

4. Suggestion Boxes and Complaints. The Culture Council will read and respond in writing to every suggestion made in your company's suggestion box. The number one reason suggestion box ideas fail is that no one responds to the suggestions as to why an idea cannot be followed up on and implemented. In our experience, there really are no suggestions that this group cannot handle; and, if they do come across a doozy, they can pass it along. Also, employee

complaints (such as parking issues or uniforms requirements, etc.) should be addressed to this group as well. **Be careful not to let this council serve as a union for your employees.** If you are building your culture correctly, this won't be a problem, especially if a lead member from the Casting Department sits on the Council.

5. Company picnics, parties, etc. These parties are currently being held. They just take on a whole new meaning when they are placed under the care of the council. These events are why you need to give the council a budget. How well they can plan is based on what they have to spend. There is nothing wrong with having fundraisers throughout the year as well to help defray the costs. One company we worked with sold electronics. The sample products were sold in a special sale, and the proceeds went to the Culture Council.

6. Sporting leagues and events. Company softball teams and bowling leagues are examples of the social (people) side of your culture and help to nurture the family environment. The more you can do, the better your company will be. Southwest Airlines and Zappos are big on these last two. They have more parties than any other company we know. Are the playing and goofing off? Their profits don't seem to say that!

Your implementation of this Culture Council will need to be early on in your culture change process. The more visible signs you can provide your employees that things are different, the faster they will adapt. The Culture Council's whole existence is about providing visible signs of your new service culture. The very fact that you have a group of employees serving the culture says it all.

You may already have a group similar to this in your organization now, and if you do, I applaud you! Many companies have employee councils or service teams in place already. You will want to re-engineer this group to fit the Culture Council format described here to take the next step to building an experience culture. This chapter is just a blueprint for you to get started. Make your Culture Council unique and put your company stamp on it. The framework provided here seeks and demands only one thing – that the Culture Council be "of service" to the culture!

The main idea of the Culture Council is that it balances the experience culture between internal and external customers. In other words, this group, while considering some customer issues, mainly focuses on the employee experience in your company. And if you are going to implement an experience culture in your company, the employee experience is paramount to your success. Treat your employees the way you want them to treat your customers. Just like in parenting, you can tell your kids what to do and what not to do, but they will always imitate you. Give your employees and experience they will want to emulate.

Reflections

What are the most important takeaways you got from this chapter?

Who else in your organization needs to read this chapter and help you create your Culture Council?

Getting to the Heart of the Matter
(Prepare for Resistance)

You can change a culture's mind fairly easily, but it's very hard to change its heart.

Resistance is futile.
- The Borg

If you are a Star Trek fan (which we already established in this book that practically everyone is), you will recognize the second quote from the biggest nemesis of the Federation – the Borg. These creatures are virtually indestructible half-human, half-android. Their goal is to take over a planet and convert all of its inhabitants to their way of life – including the reconfiguring of their bodies to be like the Borg. Whenever they would approach a spaceship or planet, they would hail them with this message "Resistance is futile." I've always loved that because it is a great message for you in your culture change efforts.

You may consider this last chapter "ending our journey on a negative," and that is certainly not my intent. As I researched, I have found that very few publications or consultants ever prepare you for the battle that is culture change. You will have your resolve tested daily during the process. The first quote in this book said, "**Culture change is not for the weak of heart!**"

In the animal kingdom, there is a type of caterpillar known as the "line" worm. This worm gets its name from its simple behavior of always following in line one behind the other. A group of scientists were fascinated by this unusual behavior and wanted to see how far the worms would take it. So they "led" the lead worm in a circle instead of a straight line so that the lead worm came up behind the last worm. And what did the lead worm do? Exactly. He started to follow the last worm in the line.

The worms would continue this circular pattern for hours. Then the scientists did an amazing thing. (Actually, it's probably the worms that were amazing.) They placed food in the middle of the ring of worms in plain sight. And the worms continued their marching following in line until – you guessed it – **they died**!

How does this relate to your company? Be careful of the line worms who will follow old systems, old processes and refuse to eat from the new "culture" even to the point of death. But that may not be so bad.

You must accept the fact now that there will be casualties.

There are people working inside your organization right now who will not like, nor will they adapt to your new experience culture. They will resist and fight you all the way until either they leave you, or you leave them. This is an unfortunate fact of culture change. It makes sense, though. When you have been involved in a project or organization outside of work, and they have decided to change the "rules," you may have decided to quit. There is nothing wrong with this. Believe it or not, there are people in this world who do not think integrity is such a great value to have. It's better to let them go than to let them damage your new company. Accept the casualty fact now or do not attempt the change.

It will be okay. What you have is a vision of tomorrow. This vision must have visible and unvisible signs for the people if they are to understand it and accept it as their own. Plan for this.

What is the Casualty Rate?

At this point I would love to say, "Here are the statistics on how many people you will lose." Unfortunately, that is not possible. There are no lines on exit interviews that ask, "Did you leave because of the culture?"—although there should be. We have no way of accounting for the reason people leave, and for the most part, people will not tell you the honest truth anyway. Remember, people draw the majority of their self-esteem from their jobs. They will fight and protect this to the death.

There are a few things we can tell you, though, to help.

1. Culture change follows the rule of thirds. A third of your people will follow you with excitement and support the change, a third will resist it, and a third will ride the fence to see who is winning and then make their decision.

2. No matter what size the company, the amount of resistance and the splits will be the same. We have studied companies with 200,000 employees to the 5,000-employee size and some with less than 20. In all cases, the distribution of reaction was the same. (My hypothesis was that the smaller the company, the easier it would be to change the culture. That idea was wrong and also number three on the list.)

3. No matter the size of your company, the culture change will be hard. Granted, the number of "converts" you have to make to your new experience culture has a direct impact on the effort of the change, but it really does not affect the difficulty of the change. Problems will surface quicker in the smaller company, but the employee will stay longer and be more challenging. We tend to find the willingness to let someone go who does not fit the culture to be almost non-existent in the smaller companies. After all, you have been working with this person for quite some time, and there is more of a family atmosphere in your company. How can you tell your "brother" that you have to let him go because he does not fit the new experience culture? Tough!

Think back to our discussions on self-esteem and culture earlier in this book. Is it any wonder we can predict the rule of thirds? The third who support you are the ones who have already separated who they are from what they do. That is why they can so easily support you. The third who rides the fence is just waiting to see who wins. Why go to all of the effort if it's all for naught? The resisting third is your outwardly vocal group. You must prepare for them. They will bolster together and try to gather support at lunch, coffee and break times. It will be informal. We have not witnessed a revolt or civil uprising from a culture change, so don't worry. But this final third will be very frustrating for you.

The two-thirds who are not fully supporting you, can you blame them? Have you introduced new policies or programs in the past only to backtrack and remove or rescind them? You know the answer is yes, so don't try to deny it. With this being the case, there is some merit to the case of the fence riders and the outright resisters. There is a chance you will change your mind. They need to know up front the difference between a culture change and introducing new parking procedures.

What I can tell you is that there are two basic approaches to changing your culture: one is the sneaky way, and one is the brass band way. I prefer the brass band way. The sneaky way is when management tries to slip in bits of culture change little by little. (Please draw your attention to exhibit 32, the culture cycle on page 74.) This little-by-little approach is so subtle that it rarely has any impact on the cycle.

You are looking for dramatic change within your organization. You have arrived at this decision based on careful analysis and study. You have also decided that this change is necessary if you are to survive. So why delay it or try to soften the blow to your company? You need it.

The best approach is the dramatic, big show method. It is sort of like setting a bomb off in the middle of your company and then rebuilding the pieces. When you use this method, you are trying to capture everyone's attention immediately. You want them to know that you are serious, this is not another fruit-of-the-month club program, and that you expect results.

At times, culture change has been likened to a chess game. Your opening move sets up your whole strategy and says a lot about how well you will do. The bottom line is how you launch your culture change is critical. Here are some rules to remember when planning your opening move:

1. **Make it an event**. Give employees plenty of notice that something new and wonderful is coming. Do not give them too much detail ahead of time. This is like the marketing we talked about in the "Creating Your Corporate University" chapter. Tease the event, but most importantly, make it an event. Hype it up and get them excited for the day.

2. **Theme the event**. All great team efforts had a rallying cry or slogan. The most important part of your advertising campaign for your company is your tagline. Why? Because it constantly reinforces who you are and what you do. (By the way, is your new tag line for the public in line with your true product?)

3. **Put something tangible in their hands day one**. This is a very common mistake companies make. They hold tremendous pep rallies with all the pyrotechnics and live music, but do nothing more than give speeches about the future. This event must be different from anything else they have experienced before if you want it to succeed.

4. **Do not expect ANY changes from your event launch**. Wouldn't you be skeptical if you were your employees? It will take time to program your experience culture. Prepare for this in advance. Do

not be discouraged if two days after your launch everything seems back to normal. It should be. Two months after the launch, well that's another story.

5. **Have a plan for your next five moves already in place before you launch.** Many companies launch well, but they get caught up in the day-to-day activities and start to let the culture change initiative slow. Prepare in advance, the first five moves you will make, including your culture training classes; your restructuring of positions if necessary; your vocabulary change; any signage that needs to change; and your training program to communicate your product, purpose, mission, and experience formula. (Do not try to do the latter all in one class by the way.)

6. **MAKE SURE CASTING (PEOPLE/HUMAN RESOURCES) IS INVOLVED!** I cannot stress this part enough. The laws of today's land favor the employee, even in the so-called "at will" employment states. When you make the decision to cut someone from the team, make sure you do it following solid coaching practices ripe with documentation. The cuts are not immediate in all cases (although your decision to cut the person is immediate). Make sure you have all of your documentation in place and all of your bases covered. The last thing you need is a wrongful termination lawsuit! The distraction alone will cost you the culture change – not to mention the financial hardship when you lose. By involving your People/Human Resources (Casting) team, you get a partner to make sure that you cover all of your bases. They know the laws and, better yet, they know what will happen regardless of the law. Use them, but do NOT let them scare you off your path. Always focus on BEHAVIOR and you'll be fine.

7. **SPEED. SPEED. SPEED.** Gradual change may seem like the right way to go, but trust us, you will lose.

Keep your pace up and rolling and do not let the negative third derail you, as they will try. Never let the bus drop below 55mph!

Never Give in to Resistance

Whatever you do, do not give into resistance! When you started this journey of building an experience culture it was with a written plan. Any deviation from this original plan during the culture change will ultimately leave you missing your mark. You will end up somewhere off to the right. Many times companies invest hundreds of thousands of dollars to change their culture, but they change their plan so many times that by the time they hit the finish line, it has moved two miles away. And suddenly, guess what? You are now ready for another culture change!

When I was helping a conference center put in a service culture, one of the ideas was to change the nametags of everyone to include their nicknames. (I briefly mentioned this example in the "Casting" chapter.)

In the travel industry, it is very common to place your hometown on the bottom of your nametag or the number of years you have been with the hotel. If you travel at all, you have seen this many times. This company wanted to do something really unique with this idea by adding the employee's nickname on their nametag.

Two months after the nametags were passed out (in a very nice ceremony, we might add), two cast members became very vocal about the nametags. So management decided to hold a meeting and vote on the nametags.

Before I go any further, some background that you need here is the response from the customer to the new nametags. It was wonderful. When a letter was sent in praising employees, the customer always mentioned them by his or her nickname instead of their real name. One manager told the story of running into someone at a convention, and that person was not sure what her real name was, but he sure remembered: "Sweet Pea"—her nickname! So the idea was working wonderfully. The problem was that there were a few "vocalizers" who personally did not care for the new nametag.

The vote caused confusion among the employees. It divided them. Obviously, the resistant third voted against them, the supportive third were all for them, but the third on the fence were afraid where to put their support and ultimately sided

"SWEET PEA"

with the resistant (vocal.) The result, management changed back to the old nametags. The damage? The people started commenting to us (including one of the customers) how different things were since they took the new nametags away. The regular customers had noticed a positive difference in the service of the conference center employees since their last visit.

The nametags were a visible sign of the new culture. Every day, each person was reminded that they were supposed to think and act differently now. Unfortunately, with this reneging of the plan, this company **had set its culture change back by six months**. "Come on. All this over a nametag?" you say. "I don't know about that!" Well, it's true.

Let's analyze this situation. What message did the nametags send to the employees? I am different. I have a role to play. What message did changing the nametags send to the employees? We are only different if the employees say so. Now, the employees of this company will not take anything else seriously. And why should they? All they have to do is complain, and they will get their way. But the ones complaining are the vocal third that will complain no matter what you do!

Never let the resistant third decide your culture.

The truth is up until now; this resistant third probably has been running your culture. These are the first steps you are taking to take control of the culture. They are not going to want to give up that control so easily.

What we will say about the conference center management staff in this story is that they had their heart in the right place. Management was trying to be empathetic to the voices of its employees. This is not something tried by most companies, so we will give them credit for that. The mistake they made was who they were trying to be empathetic towards – the resisters. **This is the wrong third to cater to.** Remember in the "Casting" chapter, what did I say to do with someone who does not like the new plan? Either recast them in another role where they will be more comfortable or move them on. The saddest part of this story is that the most vocal opponent to the nametag quit five days later anyway. If the conference center would have stuck to its plan…

Be open to resistance. Do not form the secret "culture police" whose job it is to find the resisters and convert them by any means possible or snuff them out. Let everyone know that they are entitled to their opinion, and you are happy and willing to listen. Keeping it out in the open like this actually, diffuses a lot of the resistance.

For the resistors, speed is their worst enemy. As we stated earlier, SPEED, SPEED, SPEED. (You see there is a reason I chose a bus as my analogy early on.) Actually, resisters are not trying to slow you down to mess you up; they are trying to slow you down to give themselves time to formulate a plan. If you slow the pace of change, then they are winning. The slower the change rate, the more dangerous it is for you. Keep the pace up to a speed that only allows the resistors to play catch up. When you achieve this, their impact will be minimal. This will keep them off balance and destroy the resister's campaign.

The most important thing I can leave you with is this – You must get to the heart of your culture to change it. It is very easy to get a culture to change its mind (as we saw with the nametag story); but, it is very hard to get it to change its heart. Your employees will always take the path of least resistance for themselves. It will be some time before they will take on this new vision as their own.

In the book The Day America Told the Truth, the author's research cited that 91% of all Americans admitted that they lie. It may be a small white lie to protect someone, but they did admit to some form of inconsistency with the truth. Knowing this statistic only supports the fact that your employees may not always give you the honest shake on how they are feeling at any given time during this process. Be prepared to live during that time. Here are some tips for dealing with this: (By the way, the other 9% of the people in the survey above who said they did not lie…they're lying!)

1. **Prepare your management early with what's going to happen and then remind them every week**. Your managers will hear what you are saying, but they will not understand what you mean until they start to feel it on a daily basis. The resistance and complaining will come to the managers, not the CEO. Prepare them for this carefully making sure you do not make them "gun shy."

2. **Prepare your Casting (People/Human Resources) Department**. They are most likely to receive dozens of "woe is me" talks from your employees. It is always the intention of the employee to get HR to take sides. If you do not keep them well informed on what is going on and why, they will have to choose a side on their own and believe us, the HR department in a company is usually the most damaging to a culture change effort!

3. **Let everyone know that it is going to get worse before it gets better**. There will be many battles during the early stages of your culture change. These battles could go on for as long as two years depending on the criteria listed earlier in this book. More than anything else, your role as the leader and champion of this culture change is to be a cheerleader and morale booster.

4. **NEVER take the "This is how it's going to be so if you don't like it get out!" approach**. I know that I stated resistance is futile at the beginning of this chapter, but I was tongue-in-cheek. Your 1/3rd fence rider group will test you quietly. All they are asking for is some understanding as to what is going on and why. Take the time to explain it to them, and they will come to your side. Take the older outdated approach stated above, and you are shooting yourself in the foot. It will seem to work because the people will leave your office. But what you are doing is picking a fight. And guess whose side they will be on?

5. **Prepare for customer casualties as well**. Yes, that's right. You may lose a customer or two along the way. This could be from poor service by the resistors or confusion over new policies or the gap between the times when empowerment becomes woven into the fabric of your culture, instead of a wet blanket you lay over it. Here is where we separate the weak of heart from the strong. When you lose actual business because of the culture change, everyone around you will

react, and fear will become his or her driver. If everyone knows and accepts this in advance, it will prevent a knee-jerk reaction when the time comes. These types of reactions are the ones that can crash your bus. Someone else will try to grab the wheel from you because you obviously don't know what you're doing – you just lost a customer! We know better, though, don't we?

Keep the Faith and Keep the Pace

The hardest thing for you as the driver of this culture change is the pace you must set and establish. I have supported a fast pace to help ward off the resistors, but at the same time, you must temper your efforts with patience. For many, the excitement and exhilaration of changing a corporate culture drives them enthusiastically into a pole on the side of the road.

Think of your culture change process as a flight of stairs with each floor representing one of the "stops" on your culture change journey. As you start running up that flight of stairs, your adrenaline goes wild and with the more excited you get, the more stairs you try to take at a time with each stride. Skipping one or two steps at a time may work for your journey up the stairs, but what happens during the process?

First, you get tired quickly! You find yourself out of breath and needing to stop for a moment. Your pause for breath also allows your resistors to catch their breath. Second, you have a tremendous tendency to trip. Missing just one step on your culture change journey can prove very costly.

Do not try to shortcut any of the thoughts or processes within this book. These are the steps necessary to take as a roadmap for building an experience culture. Patience is your watchword. You will be challenged daily as we have continually pointed out. But always think about the future and what is on the other side of your culture change.

And lastly, your **culture is a living, breathing, tangible part of your company.** It's not touchy-feely, immeasurable stuff placed into books by people to occupy your time. It is real. It has a real impact on your balance sheet and should be listed among your assets. It has a heart and mind of its own. Change its heart.

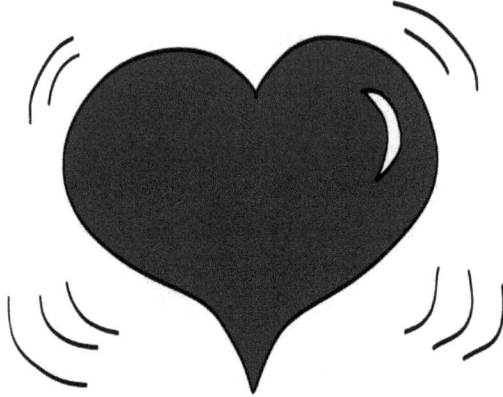

Remember the scorpion and the frog? The scorpion got the frog to change his mind, and the frog got the scorpion to change his heart—so he thought. Your current culture is like the scorpion, easy to change its mind and commit, but hard to change its heart. The scorpion's identity (its foundational beliefs and values) kicked in, and his behavior went back to the programming he had received all his life (the culture cycle).

Be very careful in proclaiming victory too early. You may see different attitudes and some different behaviors, but you are looking for long-term, lasting change. This takes time. Why all of the motivational speakers tell us it takes about 21 to 30 days to change or add a new habit, I'll never know. Especially when the habits have been in place for 20 years! Your culture's habits (which are displayed in the behaviors of your people) have been in place a long time as well. It will take time to form the new habits of your experience culture.

Expect results early, but expect true change much later. Recall the rules for how long a culture change takes. Three variables determine the amount of time to real change:

1.   The length of time current management has been in place.
2.   A number of total employees within your company.
3.   The length of time your current culture has been in place.

All of these factors are multipliers in the time equation. Be patient. Be persistent. Be courageous. Be "of service" to your people. Most importantly, lead this culture change through example.

You are about to embark on the most invigorating bus ride of your professional life. Embrace it. Enjoy it. It will be equal parts exhilarating and frustrating. But your very business life depends on its success.

Take your time in the Design Phase. Get the right people on the bus. And then DRIVE! I will be the one holding the "you can do it!" sign along the road as you whiz by. I might even say it aloud in my best Rob Schneider voice (see "The Waterboy" to get that final joke.)

Break a Leg!

Postlude

The following is my favorite Disney story about Walt and his legacy told to us, by the way, by a front-line cast member.

> Walt died in 1966 several years before the completion of EPCOT center in Orlando, Florida. On the night before his death, he stared at the diagram of the park and gave instructions to his brother Roy concerning his vision. EPCOT was to be the futuristic city of tomorrow. It was Walt's vision of the future. At the dedication and opening ceremony of EPCOT, Lillian, Walt's wife was asked to cut the ribbon and say a few words. The reporters crowded around her and barraged her with questions. One reporter gesturing to the grand crowds and beautiful structures of EPCOT center asked, "Mrs. Disney, isn't it sad that Walt was not here to see all this?" Lillian looked at the reporter and smilingly said, "Honey, Walt saw all this first!"

There will probably never be a better story told on the power of vision. We want this to be your first thought as you start on your journey and the last thought when you finish this book. And if you get discouraged through your process, just turn to this page and read this story again and again. The moral is simple. You have a vision for what your company can and will become. Your company has a purpose for its existence. Along the way, you will be called a dreamer, an un-realist, and more. But remember all the negative things people said about Walt Disney while he was building his vision and know that when you get on the other side, the reporters will be there waiting and so will I!

About Matt

For the past 30 years, Matthew Hudson has made his living as a retail artist. Along the way, he has won many awards for his intuitive concepts and creative ideas and been published several times. He has a PhD in Organizational Behavior and is a sought after speaker with a gift for bringing light to the complex. His clients include companies such as Hyatt Regency, Disney, Exxon, AmerisrouceBergen, Coton Colors, The Norman Vincent Peale Foundation, and much more. He is president of two charitable organizations, and has served on the board of several others. (Oh, and of course, the founder of @hudsonhead) He is available for consulting and speaking engagements. Contact him at matt@hudsonhead.com

A ton of change has happened since I first wrote this book years ago. But the principles and truths have remained the same. I want to thank Catherine, Madeline, Ray, Ben for their encouragement and support and my sister Mindy for inspiring me to rewrite Culturrifc! for today's generations and companies. Please accept my thanks for reading this work. I truly hope it inspires you and serves as a roadmap for your organization – whether for-profit or non-profit. And please remember – all truth is God's truth!

- Matt

Go to hudsonhead.com to order other books by Matt

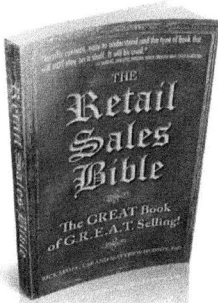

The Retail Sales Bible
The G.R.E.A.T. Selling System for Retail.
Written for retail sales professionals.
$19.95

Advisor Selling
The art and science of becoming a trusted sales
advisor. Written for outside sales reps.
$19.95

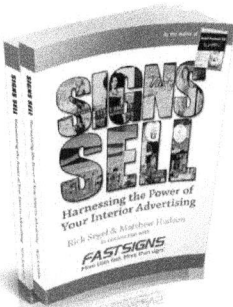

Signs Sell
Harnessing the Power of Your Interior
Advertising (full color)
$25.95

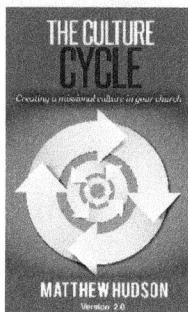

The Culture Cycle (e-book)
Creating a missional culture in your church.
$1.95

www.ingramcontent.com/pod-product-compliance
Lightning Source LLC
Chambersburg PA
CBHW060326200326
41519CB00011BA/1848